My Second
Picture Dictionary

by Hale C. Reid
Helen W. Crane
Betty Ellen Jenkins

Illustrations by Tom Cooke *and* Bea Holmes

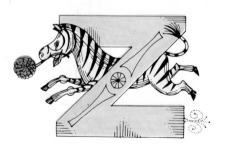

Silver Burdett & Ginn

To the Boys and Girls Who Use This Book

Welcome to MY SECOND PICTURE DICTIONARY. This book has two parts. The first part has words and meanings. The second part has lists of special words. Both parts have many colorful pictures.

The first part lists words in alphabetical order. These words are printed in dark type. They are called *entry words*. What are the entry words on page 1?

Beside most entry words is the definition, or meaning. What is the definition for the word **hat** on page 64?

Below the definition for each entry word is a sentence or a group of sentences. The sentences show you ways the entry word can be used. On page 14, read the sentences for the word **boat**.

Some entry words are printed in two or more parts. Each part is called a *syllable*. What are the syllables in the word **today**? In writing you can divide a word between syllables at the end of a line. Where would you divide the word **today** at the end of a line?

Often there is a small mark (') following a syllable. This mark is called a *stress mark*. It shows you which syllable you should speak louder. Where would the stress mark be in the word **today**?

Sometimes an entry word has a direction instead of a definition. Look up the word **ate**. Follow the direction and see what you find. Now look up the word **lion**. What do you find when you follow the direction?

The second part of the dictionary has lists of words. In each list the words are in alphabetical order and are related to one another. Find page 189. What lists follow this page?

We hope that you will enjoy using MY SECOND PICTURE DICTIONARY to learn about words.

The Authors

0-663-42380-5

Contents

	PAGE
To the Boys and Girls Who Use This Book	ii
Do You Know?	iv
Words and Definitions	1
Word Lists	189
Words for the Space Age	190
Compound Words	191
Antonyms (Word Opposites)	192
Homonyms	193
Kinds of Workers	194
Words for Flowers	196
Words for Fruits	198
Words for Vegetables	200
Words for Animals	202
Birds	211
Dogs	214
Words for Colors	216
Number Words	217
The Days of the Week	217
The Months and Some Important Days	218
To Parents and Teachers	220

Do You Know?

Look at the forms of the letter A at the top of page 1. Do you know the names of the two animals pictured with the letters? With what letter does each animal's name begin? As you use this dictionary, see if you know the names of the other animals and objects shown with the letters at the beginning of each section. The list below will help you review the alphabet and name the pictures.

A a	alligator, ant		N n	newsboy, newspapers
B b	boy, butterfly, balloon		O o	octopus, orchid
C c	caterpillar, cap		P p	parrot
D d	donkey, daisies		Q q	question mark
E e	elf, Easter egg		R r	rooster, robin
F f	farmer, frog, flowers		S s	sailor, soda, straw
G g	girl, glasses		T t	tiger, trumpet
H h	hippopotamus, hat		U u	unicorn, umbrella
I i	Indian		V v	violinist
J j	jack-in-the-box		W w	walrus, watch
K k	kangaroo, kite		X x	xylophone
L l	lion, lorgnette		Y y	yak, yo-yo
M m	moose, mirror		Z z	zebra, zinnia

a   any; one
        Do you have **a** dollar?
        A sunny day makes me feel happy.

about   having to do with; almost; around
        Bill wrote a story **about** animals.
        The time is **about** two o'clock.
        The boat bounced **about** on the lake.

above   higher than; over
        The red books are **above** the blue
        books in the bookcase.
        Our apartment is **above** a store.

across   on the other side of; from one side to the
        other
        The city is **across** the river.
        The dog ran **across** the road.

afraid   feeling fear
        The mouse is **afraid** of the cat.

af′ ter   later than; following
        Darkness comes **after** daylight.
        We played ball **after** school.

af ter noon' the time between noon and evening
It rained all **afternoon,** but it was clear by night.

again once more
I want to read that story **again.**

against upon or touching; on the opposite side of
The bat is **against** the wall.
His team plays **against** my team.

ahead in front
The car is **ahead** of the truck.
Jim ran **ahead** of the other boys.

air the mixture of gases around the earth
The **air** is warmer today.

air' plane a flying machine which is heavier than air and which is driven by a propeller or jet power
An **airplane** has wings.

air' port a place where airplanes can land and take off
There is an airplane at the **airport.**

all every part of; every one of
The kitten drank **all** the milk.
All dogs have ears.

al' li ga tor   *See* **Words for Animals,** page 202.

al' most   nearly
I am **almost** ready.

alone   without any other person; by oneself
Betty is walking **alone.**

along   from one end to another
Many trees grow **along** our street.
I walked **along** the sidewalk.

al' so   too; in addition
I brushed my hair. I **also** combed it.

al' ways   at all times
Tuesday **always** comes after Monday.

am   a form that is used with the word *I* to
show present time
I **am** a child.
I **am** using a dictionary.

Amer' i ca   the United States; North America and
Amer' i can South America
America is my country.
I live in North **America.**
I am an **American.**

an   any; one
An elephant is **an** animal.

and   as well as; added to

Apples **and** oranges are fruits.

Three **and** two are five.

an' gry   feeling cross

I was **angry** because Ed hit my dog.

an' i mal   a living thing that moves about by itself

A dog is an **animal.**

an oth' er   one more; a different

May I have **another** ride?

Mary has gone to **another** school.

an' swer   the word you say or write when you are asked a question

Richard gave the best **answer** to Miss Cook's question.

ant   *See* **Words for Animals,** page 202.

an' te lope   *See* **Words for Animals,** page 202.
  an' te lope or **an' te lopes**

a ny   one out of many; some

You may come **any** time you wish.

Have you **any** money?

See **Words for Fruits,** page 198.

apri cot   *See* **Words for Fruits,** page 198.

are   a form that is used to show present
                time (Use with *you, we, they,* and words
                that mean more than one.)
                    Are you ready? We **are** ready.
                    Jane and Mary **are** sisters.
                    The boys **are** swimming.

arm   the part of the body between the shoulder
                and the hand
                    The little girl is raising her **arm.**

around   in a circle; on every side of; in an
                opposite direction
                    The top is spinning **around.**
                    We walked **around** the block.
                    Please turn **around.**

as   equally; while
                    I am **as** tall as my brother.
                    It began to rain **as** we were eating.

ask   to try to find out by using words
                    I will **ask** Miss Woods the answer to
                the question.

asleep   sleeping
                    Joanne is **asleep.**

as par′ a gus *See* **Words for Vegetables,** page 200.

as′ ter   *See* **Words for Flowers,** page 196.

as′ tro naut   a person who travels in a spaceship

The **astronaut** is wearing a space suit for the space flight.

at   in; on; when the time is

Janet is **at** school.
Tina was waiting **at** the corner.
I eat breakfast **at** seven o'clock.

ate   *See* **eat.**

au′ di ence   a group of people who hear or see

A man is speaking to the **audience.**
The **audience** is listening to him.

aunt   a sister of one's father or mother; the wife of one's uncle

My mother's sister is my **aunt.**

au′ thor   a person who writes books or stories

Who is the **author** of the book?

au′ tumn   the season between summer and winter; fall

Some trees lose their leaves in the **autumn.**

awake   not asleep

Kim is **awake,** but Chris is asleep.

away   from a place; at a distance

Mary is **away** at camp.
Stay **away** from the river.

ba′ by
ba′ bies
a young child
Our **baby** is learning to crawl.

back
the upper part of the body opposite the front part; the opposite of *front*
Tom is lying on his **back.**
Philip sits in the **back** of the room.

bad
not good
We played indoors because the weather was **bad.**
Sally has a **bad** cold.

bag
a sack or container which is made of cloth, paper, leather, or plastic; a traveling case; a pocketbook
The marbles are in a **bag.**
Father put the **bag** in the car.
Mrs. Roberts has a blue **bag.**

bake
bak′ ing
to cook by dry heat, usually in an oven
Mother will **bake** a cake in the oven.
The cook was **baking** a pie.

ball something that is round; a game in which a ball is used
> Here is a **ball** of string.
> Most boys like to play **ball**.

ball a large party or dance
> Cinderella danced at the **ball**.

bal loon' a bag which can be blown up with air
> A **balloon** is often made of thin rubber.

ba nana *See* **Words for Fruits,** page 198.

bank a place to keep money
> I put my money in the **bank**.

bark the covering of a tree
> The trunk and branches of the tree are covered with **bark**.

bark the sharp cry of a dog
> The dog's **bark** is loud.

barn a large building for storing farm crops and keeping farm animals
> The farmer stores hay in his **barn**.

base' ball a game played with a bat and a ball by two teams; the ball used in the game
> Many boys play **baseball**.
> The pitcher threw the **baseball**.

base′ ment   the room below the first floor of a
building, sometimes below ground
There is a washing machine in the
basement.

bas′ ket   something, often made by weaving, which
is used for carrying or holding things
We filled the **basket** with apples.

bat   a stick used to hit the ball in baseball
We play baseball with a **bat.**

bat   *See* **Words for Animals,** page 202.

bath   the washing of the body
I took a **bath** in the bathtub.

be   I will **be** here at ten o'clock.
  been   Anne and Sue have **been** to the library.
  be′ ing   The children are **being** quiet.

bean   *See* **Words for Vegetables,** page 200.

bear   *See* **Words for Animals,** page 202.

beat   to hit again and again; to do better than;
  beat   to mix by stirring quickly
  beat′ en   The boy **beats** the drum.
Our team **beat** their team last week.
The cook has **beaten** the eggs.

beau' ti ful   very pretty to see or hear
         I picked a **beautiful** flower.

bea' ver   *See* **Words for Animals,** page 202.

be cause'   for the reason that
         Our grass is brown, **because** we have not had rain.

be come'   to come to be; to happen to
  be came'   Some seeds **become** plants.
  be come'   What **became** of the popcorn?
  be com' ing   The girl has **become** a dancer.
         The weather is **becoming** warmer.

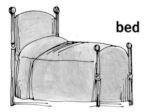

bed   something which is used to sleep on; a piece of ground where plants are grown
         I sleep in a **bed.**
         Flowers are growing in the flower **bed.**

bee   *See* **Words for Animals,** page 202.

been   *See* **be.**

beet   *See* **Words for Vegetables,** page 200.

bee' tle   *See* **Words for Animals,** page 202.

be fore'   in front of; earlier than; earlier
         The pilot is standing **before** the class.
         Before school, Tim played marbles.
         I have read this book **before.**

be gin′   to start

    be gan′   When do the races **begin**?

    be gun′   It **began** to snow.

    be gin′ ning   The teams have **begun** the game.

                   Leaves are **beginning** to fall.

be hind′   at the back of; late

                Mike sits **behind** Martha.

                The students are **behind** in their work.

be lieve′   to think something is true or real; to feel
sure

         I **believe** what she says.

         I **believe** I can do that.

bell   a hollow metal cup that rings when
struck by a kind of hammer

         Did someone ring the **bell**?

be low′   lower than; beneath or under

         The temperature is **below** zero.

         The subway runs **below** the street.

be side′   at the side of; close to

         The table is **beside** the chair.

         Stand **beside** me.

be sides′   in addition to

         Many people **besides** Chris were late.

best   *See* **good** *and* **well.**

bet′ ter   *See* **good** *and* **well.**

be tween′   in the space from one object, person, or time to another; from each of
    Sue is sitting **between** Mother and Father.
    We came **between** one and two o'clock.
    Between us, Pat and I had a dollar.

bi′ cy cle   something to ride which has two wheels, one behind the other
    I rode my **bicycle** to school.

big   large
  big′ ger   Joan caught a **big** fish.
  big′ gest   The fish Mary caught was **bigger** than Joan's.
    Paul caught the **biggest** fish of all.

bird   *See* **Birds,** page 211.

birth′ day   the day of the year on which a person was born
    My **birthday** is in May.

bite   •the amount of something which is bitten off by the teeth; a cut made by the teeth
    Ronnie took a **bite** of the apple.
    Ruth has a dog **bite** on her hand.

  •to cut into with the teeth; to sting
  bit   I hope the dog doesn't **bite** me.
  bit′ ten   A mosquito **bit** Kim.
  bit′ ing   Who has **bitten** into this apple?
    The cold wind is **biting** my cheeks.

black' ber ry *See* **Words for Fruits, page 198.**
  black' ber ries

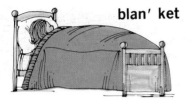

blan' ket a cover for a bed, often made of wool or cotton; a thick covering
  The girl is sleeping under a warm **blanket.**
  A **blanket** of snow covered the earth.

blew *See* **blow.**

block a thick piece of something, such as wood; the space between streets in a city or a town
  Joe is playing with a wooden **block.**
  Does Pam live in this **block**?

blood the liquid that flows through the arteries and veins in one's body
  There is some **blood** on the girl's cut finger.

blos' som a flower, especially of a plant or a tree which bears fruit
  Here is an apple **blossom.**

blow to make air move; to move by the force
  blew of air
  blown Our dog howls when the wind **blows.**
  blow' ing Dust **blew** into my eyes.
  Someone's hat had **blown** away.
  A gentle breeze is **blowing.**

blow   a hard hit
              He got a bump from the hard **blow.**

blue′ ber ry   *See* **Words for Fruits,** page 198.
blue′ ber ries

board   a thin, flat piece of wood
              The men nailed **boards** together to
              build a fence.

board   to get on a train, ship, or plane
              Every day many people **board** the
              train for the city.

boat   an object used for traveling on water
              A red **boat** is near the shore.
              A **boat** with a sail is in the lake.

body   the whole person or animal; the main
bod′ ies part
              A cat's **body** is covered with fur.
              The **body** of the letter tells about
              Jim's trip.

book   sheets of paper held together at one side
              and often printed on
              I am reading a story in a **book.**

boot   a thick covering for the foot and part of
              the leg
              This **boot** is made of red rubber.

born   given birth to
                 Many babies are **born** every day.

both   the two
                 Both girls have red hair.
                 Both of them are smiling.

bot′ tle   a container which is usually made of glass
                 and which has a narrow neck or opening
                 We filled the **bottle** with water.

bot′ tom   the lowest part
                 A house is at the **bottom** of the hill.
                 The letter dropped to the **bottom** of
                 the mailbox.

bought   *See* **buy.**

bounce   to spring like a rubber ball
bounc′ ing   The baby likes to **bounce** on his
                 father's knee.
                 The ball was **bouncing** down the stairs.

bowl   a round, deep dish
                 Mother beats eggs in a **bowl.**

bowl   to play a game in which one rolls a ball
                 down an alley at something such as a
                 wooden pin
                 Father and Bill **bowl** at the bowling
                 alley.

box
box' es
a wooden or cardboard form to hold things
> I'll put the papers in this **box.**

boy
a male child
> The **boy** will someday be a man.

branch
branch' es
a part of a tree, growing out from the trunk and above the ground; a part that is joined to the main part
> A bird is sitting on the **branch.**

brave
not afraid to face danger
> The fireman is **brave.**

brave
a North American Indian fighter
> The **brave** is wearing feathers.

bread
a baked food which is made with flour and other things
> Mother bought a loaf of fresh **bread** at the bakery.

break
broke
bro' ken
break' ing
to make something come apart; to come apart
> Should I **break** the candy in half?
> The string on the package **broke.**
> The pipe has **broken** in two places.
> Some men are **breaking** up pieces of wood for the fire.

break' fast   the early morning meal
We eat **breakfast** before we leave for
school.

breeze   a light wind
The **breeze** feels cool.

brick   a block of baked clay used for building
Brick is used to make many chimneys.

bridge   something built to carry a road over
water, railroad tracks, or another road
The cars got to the other side of the
river by driving across the **bridge.**

bright   shining; cheerful; having a quick mind
The sun is **bright.**
She has a **bright** smile.
Jane's answers show that she is a
bright child.

bring
brought
bring' ing

to come with something from another
place
I will **bring** you a drink of water.
The postman **brought** a letter.
Harry is **bringing** a rabbit to school.

broc' co li   See **Words for Vegetables,** page 200.

broke   See **break.**

brook a small stream of water
Mark caught a fish in the **brook.**

broth′ er a boy or a man who has the same mother
and father that another person has
Tom has one **brother** and two sisters.

brought *See* **bring.**

brush ● a tool with hair or wires set in a handle
brush′ es I need a **brush** for painting.

● to use a brush
How often do you **brush** your teeth?
Joan **brushes** her hair every day.

brush low bushes and trees
The **brush** is thick in the woods.

buck′ et a round, deep container with a handle
The **bucket** is full of sand.

buf′ fa lo *See* **Words for Animals,** page 203.
buf′ fa lo or **buf′ fa loes**

bug a crawling and sometimes flying insect
A tiny **bug** was on the pumpkin leaf.

build to make by putting parts together
built Carpenters **build** houses.
build′ ing Teddy **built** a fort with his blocks.
I am **building** a toy airplane.

build' ing   a place which has walls and a roof
                   Our school is a large **building.**

bump   ● a swelling caused by hitting; a raised
             place
                   The **bump** on my head hurts.
                   The car shook as it went over a **bump.**

             ● to push or to hit
                   Babies may **bump** into things when
             they are learning to walk.

bunch   a group of things of the same kind
bunch' es   This is a **bunch** of grapes.

burn   to be on fire; to set on fire
                   The logs **burn** in the fireplace.
                   Forest fires **burn** many trees.

bus   a large automobile for carrying many
bus' es or passengers
bus'ses   The **bus** travels across town.

bush   a plant which is smaller than a tree and
bush' es   which has many stems
                   Blueberries grow on a **bush.**

business   work
                   What is your father's **business**?

busy   active; at work

A police officer stands at the **busy** street corner.

Mother is **busy** writing a book.

but   however; except

I wanted to go, **but** I was sick.

Everyone is here **but** Sandy.

but′ ter   a food which is made from cream

I like to put **butter** on rolls.

but′ ter fly   *See* **Words for Animals,** page 203.
  but′ ter flies

but′ ton   a round, flat object which is used on clothing

You fasten your coat by putting the **button** through the buttonhole.

buy   to get by paying a certain price
  bought
  buy′ ing

We **buy** eggs at the store.

Rita **bought** an apple for a quarter.

It is raining, and people are **buying** umbrellas.

by   near; through the means of; in a measure of; no later than

Lisa lives **by** the new highway.

Mrs. Forest travels **by** airplane.

We get milk **by** the gallon.

By noon the rain had stopped.

cab′ bage	*See* **Words for Vegetables,** page 200.

cab′ in	a small, simple house usually built of wood; a room on a ship The **cabin** is made of logs. A person sleeps in a **cabin** on a ship.

cage	a place closed in by bars where birds or animals are kept The parrot is in a **cage.**

cake	a baked mixture of flour, eggs, sugar, and other things; a solid piece of food or other material Many people like chocolate **cake.** I bought a **cake** of soap.

calf **calves**	*See* **Words for Animals,** page 203.

call	to shout; to name Did you hear someone **call**? I **call** my cat Whiskers.

came	*See* **come.**

cam′ el   *See* **Words for Animals,** page 203.

cam′ era   a tight box for taking pictures
                   This **camera** takes good pictures.

camp   a group of tents or cabins for outdoor
                   living; a place where people live for a
                   short time
                        Tim is going to summer **camp.**
                        There is a trailer **camp** outside the
                   city.

can   to be able to; may
  could   Molly **can** run fast.
                        I **can** play with you.
                        Kate **could** swim before I could.

can   a container made of metal
                        John opened a **can** of soup.
                        Art threw the rags in the trash **can.**

can′ dle   a stick of wax with a wick that gives off
                   light as it burns
                        The **candle** is lighted.

can′ dy   sugar and other things boiled with water
  can′ dies   and made into pieces for eating
                        That **candy** tastes like real fruit.

can′ not   not to be able to
                        I **cannot** see when my eyes are shut.

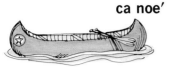

ca noe'   a light boat which is moved with paddles
A **canoe** is a narrow boat.

can' ta loupe *See* **Words for Fruits,** page 198.

can' yon   a long valley with steep sides, usually with water at the bottom
A **canyon** may be hundreds of feet deep.

cap   a small, close-fitting head cover; a cover for a bottle
Jack will put the **cap** on his head.
Will you take the **cap** off the bottle?

car   an automobile; an object that moves on four wheels and often carries something
The man is driving the **car.**
The railroad **car** is on the track.

card   a flat piece of stiff paper with many uses
A letter is on each alphabet **card.**
Patty made a birthday **card.**
The directions are written on a blue **card.**

care
car' ing   to be troubled about one's needs; to have an interest for
Mother cats **care** for their kittens.
Do you **care** for any dessert?
Jill is **caring** for the children.

care′ ful   watchful
  care′ ful ly   Be **careful** when you cross the street.
               John works **carefully.**

car na′ tion   *See* **Words for Flowers,** page 196.

car′ rot   *See* **Words for Vegetables,** page 200.

car′ ry   to take something from one place to
  car′ ries   another
  car′ ried   I will **carry** the suitcase.
  car′ ry ing   This train **carries** passengers.
               Father **carried** the sick boy.
               That airplane is **carrying** mail.

cas′ tle   a large building with thick walls and
          towers
            An old **castle** stood on the hill.

cat   *See* **Words for Animals,** page 203.

catch   to get hold of
  catch′ es   Let Jack **catch** the football.
  caught   One of the players **catches** the ball.
  catch′ ing   The cat **caught** a mouse last night.
            Are you **catching** any fish?

catch′ er   one who catches something in a game
            The **catcher** is a good player.

cat′ tle   cows and steers
            The **cattle** are in the barn.

caught   *See* **catch.**

cau' li flow er   *See* **Words for Vegetables,** page 200.

cave   a space underground
                 It is dark inside the **cave.**

cel' ery   *See* **Words for Vegetables,** page 200.

cent   a penny; a piece of money
                 Marcia paid one **cent** for a piece of
                 gum.

chair   a seat for one person
                 Goldilocks sat in the **chair.**

change   • money returned to you when you have
                 paid more than something cost; coins
                    The grocer gave me a dime in **change.**
                    Father has a pocketful of **change.**

                 • to make different; to become different;
                 to go from one thing to another
chang' ing   Should I **change** my drawing?
                    The weather may **change** from cloudy
                 to sunny.
                    Joan is **changing** her clothes.

chase   to go after to catch
  chas' ing   For fun, the boys **chase** each other
                 around the yard.
                    Some dogs were **chasing** cars.

chat′ ter   to talk fast; to make sounds that are like language
> Listen to the children **chatter.**
> Squirrels often **chatter** to themselves.

cheese   a food made from the thick part of milk
> May I have a piece of **cheese**?

cher′ ry   *See* **Words for Fruits,** page 198.
  cher′ ries

chick′ en   *See* **Words for Animals,** page 203.

chief   the person who leads a group
> The police **chief** is an important man.

child   a young boy or girl
  chil′ dren
> Each **child** is going to school.
> You are your parents' **child.**
> A **child** grows every day.

chilly   cold
> The wind is **chilly** today.

chim′ ney   something to carry smoke away from a building
> The **chimney** is on the roof.

chim pan zee′ *See* **Words for Animals,** page 203.

chip′ munk   *See* **Words for Animals,** page 203.

choc′ o late   a food that is made from the seeds of a plant and used in cooking
  Chocolate is often dark brown and sweet.

church
church′ es   a building where people worship
  My aunt was married in a **church.**

cir′ cle   a closed line that is shaped like a ring; a ring
  I drew a **circle** with my pencil.
  The children sat in a **circle.**

cir′ cus
cir′ cus es   a show of clowns, acrobats, and animals
  There may be dancing elephants at the **circus.**
  The **circus** is exciting to watch.

city
cit′ ies   a large important town where many people live
  There are many businesses in the **city.**

clam   *See* **Words for Animals,** page 203.

clean   • free from dirt
  I wash my hands to get them **clean.**

  • to take away dirt; to make neat
  We **clean** our desks before vacation.

clear
clear' ly

easy to see through or to understand
The air is **clear.**
Her directions were **clear.**
She speaks **clearly.**

climb

to go up, often with the help of the hands and feet
Jerry can **climb** the tree.
Roses **climb** the fence in the garden.

clock

something which is used to measure and to show time
A **clock** is not carried or worn by a person as a watch is.

close
clos' ing

to shut
Judy will **close** and lock the door.
The guard is **closing** the gate.

close

near; with little space between
We live **close** to school.
The children stood **close** together.

cloth

material made from cotton, wool, and other threads
My jacket is made of red **cloth.**
He cleaned the window with a **cloth.**

clothes

coverings worn on the body
Father hung the **clothes** on the line.
People around the world wear many kinds of **clothes.**

cloud   a white or gray mass in the air which is made up of tiny drops of water
There is a puffy **cloud** in the sky.

clown   a person whose job is making people laugh
The **clown** has a pie on her head.

club
- a heavy stick of wood which is thicker at one end
  In the story the giant carried a strong **club**.

- a group of people with the same interest
  We are starting a nature **club**.

coat   clothing to wear outdoors; a thin layer that covers something
In winter I wear a **coat**.
Mother gave the door a **coat** of paint.

cold
- a sickness which often causes a running nose and a sore throat
  Chris is sick with a **cold**.

- without heat
  Ice is **cold**.

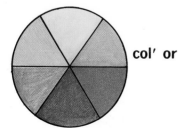

col′ or   red, yellow, blue, and the mixtures of them
Each part of the wheel is a different **color**.

come   to move toward; to happen
 came   Will you **come** to the store with me?
 come   His birthday **came** on a Friday.
 com′ ing   Who has **come** to dinner?
       The circus is **coming** to our town.

com′ pa ny friends or relatives who visit you; a
com′ pa nies business group
       We have **company** at our house.
       Father works for the bus **company.**

cone   a shape that has a round base and that
      narrows to a point at the top; the seed on
      pine, cedar, and other evergreen trees
       An ice cream **cone** has its point at the
      bottom.
       Paul found a pine **cone** in the yard.

con′ so nant any one of the letters of the alphabet
      besides the vowels which are $a, e, i, o,$
      and $u;$ a sound that stands for one of the
      consonant letters
       The letter b is a **consonant.**
       You can hear only one **consonant** in
      the word $eight.$

cook′ ie   a small flat cake
 or   David ate a **cookie** which Mother had
cooky   baked.

cool   not warm; only somewhat cold
       I wear a sweater if the air is **cool.**

corn	*See* **Words for Vegetables,** page 200.

cor′ ner   the place where two lines, sides, or
streets meet
> A ball is near the **corner** of a room.
> A **corner** of the page was torn.
> Tim Hall lives on the **corner** of the
street.

cot′ ton   a plant which has soft puffs around its
seeds; the cloth which is made from this
plant
> Some farmers raise **cotton.**
> The cloth in my dress is **cotton.**

could   *See* **can.**

count   to say the words for numbers in order; to
find out how many
> My little brother can **count** to ten.
> The teacher will **count** the children.

coun′ try
coun′ tries   land where people do not live close to
one another; the land where one lives
> June lives in the city, but her uncle
lives in the **country.**
> The United States of America is our
country.

cous′ in   the child of an aunt or an uncle
> Aunt Mary's baby is my **cousin.**

cov′ er   • a part that fits over something
A blanket is a **cover** for a bed.

• to spread over
Does the snow **cover** the rooftops?

cow   See **Words for Animals,** page 204.

cow′ boy   a man who takes care of cattle and works
on a cattle ranch
The **cowboy** is roping the calf.

coy o′ te   See **Words for Animals,** page 204.

crab   See **Words for Animals,** page 204.

crack   • a thin break
There is a **crack** in this cup.

• to snap or to break with a quick sound
The glass may **crack** if you drop it.

crash   • a sudden, loud noise
crash′ es   What made that loud **crash**?

• to make a loud noise; to smash noisily
Thunder may **crash** during a storm.
A dropped glass often **crashes** on the
floor.

cream   the yellow, fatty part of milk
             Butter is made from **cream.**

creek   a small stream of water
             We wade in the **creek** near the farm.

crick′ et   *See* **Words for Animals,** page 204.

cro′ cus   *See* **Words for Flowers,** page 196.
  cro′ cus es

crop   the amount of grain, fruit, or vegetables
             grown in a season or a year
             We have a big apple **crop** this year.

cross   ● a + or † shape
  cross′ es   Our first-aid box has a red **cross** on
             the cover.

             ● to go to the other side of
             We **cross** the street at the corner.
             The bus **crosses** the bridge.

             ● not pleased; angry
             Mother was **cross** because Jackie was
             late for dinner.

crowd   a group of many people
             There was such a **crowd** at the ball
             game that there were no empty seats.

crown   a covering for the head, worn by a king
              or a queen
                  The queen wore a **crown** of gold.

cry   to shout; to make a noise from sadness
  cries   or pain, usually with tears
  cried   You should **cry** for help if you are in
  cry′ ing trouble.
                  An unhappy person sometimes **cries**.
                  "Wait for me," Pat **cried** to the girls.
                  The baby is **crying**.

cube   a solid shape with six square sides
                  The block in the picture is shaped
              like a **cube**.

cu′ cum ber *See* **Words for Vegetables**, page 201.

cup   a small bowl with a handle which is
              used for drinking
                  Fill the **cup** with milk.

cut   ● an opening made by something sharp
                  Carol has a **cut** on her knee.

              ● to remove or to open with something
                sharp; to shorten
  cut   Mary will **cut** a picture from the
  cut′ ting newspaper with scissors.
                  Yesterday I **cut** my finger with a knife.
                  Pat is **cutting** the grass.

daf′ fo dil   *See* **Words for Flowers,** page 196.

dai′ sy   *See* **Words for Flowers,** page 196.
  dai′ sies

dance   to move the body and the feet in time to
  danc′ ing   music; to move quickly as if to music
      I like to **dance.**
      Leaves were **dancing** in the breeze.

dan′ ger ous   causing trouble or harm
      Sharp knives may be **dangerous.**

dark   with little or no light; deep in color
      The house is **dark** without lights.
      Her eyes are **dark** brown.

date   *See* **Words for Fruits,** page 198.

day   the time when it is light between sunrise
      and sunset; a measure of time, about
      twenty-four hours long
      This has been a sunny **day.**
      Sunday is the first **day** of the week.

dead   without life
            These flowers are **dead.**

dear   greatly loved
            She is my **dear** friend.

deep   far below the top
            Parts of the ocean are very **deep.**

deer   *See* **Words for Animals,** page 204.
  deer

de gree' a point used in measuring
            It is one **degree** below zero.

des' ert a hot, sandy region with little water
            Days are hot in the **desert.**

des sert' sweets served at the end of a meal
            We had apple pie for **dessert.**

did   *See* **do.**

die   to lose life
  dy' ing   If an animal doesn't eat for a long
            time, he may **die.**
            The rose bush is **dying.**

dif' fer ent not alike; not the same
            A square is **different** from a circle.
            We saw Mary three **different** times.

dig   to use hands or tools to make a hole
  dug   Our dog likes to **dig.**
  dig′ ging   He **dug** a large hole last week.
               Now he is **digging** in the garden.

dime   money worth ten cents
               Ted gave me a **dime** for ten pennies.

din′ ner   the main meal of the day, which is served
               at noon or in the evening
               The Greens eat **dinner** at noon.

di′ no saur   *See* **Words for Animals,** page 204.

di rec′ tion   an order or a rule for doing something; the
line or way toward which a person or thing
can go
      I'll read the first **direction** for making
the cookies.
      A compass shows the **direction** in
which you are facing.

dirt   earth or soil
  dirty   We plant seeds in **dirt.**
             My hands are **dirty.**

dish   a container for holding food
  dish′ es   Elsa will put the carrots in a **dish.**

ditch   a long, narrow place dug in the ground
  ditch′ es   Sometimes there is water in a **ditch.**
            Men dug a **ditch** along the road.

dive   to go headfirst into the water
  dived or   Nancy can **dive** well.
  dove   Al **dived** from the high diving board.
  div′ ing   Jan is **diving** into the pool.

do   to perform; to carry through on a job
  does   The dog can **do** a funny trick.
  did   Mary **does** her work well.
  done   John **did** his work this morning.
  do′ ing   I have **done** my arithmetic.
                      What are you **doing**?

dog   See **Dogs,** page 214.

doll   a toy made to look like a person or an animal
                      My **doll** looks like a little girl.

dol′ lar   a piece of money worth one hundred pennies
                      Frank earned a **dollar.**

dol′ phin   See **Words for Animals,** page 204.

done   See **do.**

don′ key   See **Words for Animals,** page 204.

door   a part which can be moved to close an opening in a wall; the opening in a wall through which people walk
                      Lock the **door** so that it will not open.
                      Father had just walked in the **door.**

down   to a lower place
                We walked **down** the long hill.

dream   the thoughts or pictures that are in a
                person's mind when asleep
                I had a funny **dream.**

dress   ● a piece of clothing worn by girls and
  dress' es women
                Sue is wearing a red **dress** with a full
              skirt.

           ●to put on clothes
                We **dress** warmly in cold weather.
                Mary **dresses** for school before she
              eats breakfast.

drink   to swallow liquid
  drank   I **drink** milk with every meal.
  drunk   Jill **drank** two glasses of water.
  drink' ing Who has **drunk** from this cup?
                They are **drinking** lemonade.

drive   to make go
  drove   **Drive** the nail into the board with the
  driv' en hammer.
  driv' ing Mrs. Rose once **drove** a truck.
                The noise has **driven** the dog away.
                A farmer is **driving** a team of horses.

driv' er   a person who makes something, such as
                a car, go
                Mr. Gordon is the **driver** of the bus.

drop   • a small amount of liquid, often with a
                  round shape
                     A **drop** of water is on the faucet.

                • to fall; to let fall
dropped   The loose button may **drop** off your
drop′ ping coat.
                     Laura **dropped** the letter.
                     The temperature is **dropping.**

drove   *See* **drive.**

drum   a musical instrument which makes a
                sound when beaten
                     Use the sticks to beat the **drum.**

dry   • without liquid; not wet
                     The earth on the desert is **dry.**

                • to remove water from; to lose water
dries   I will **dry** the dishes.
dried   After a rainstorm the sidewalk **dries.**
dry′ ing   The wet shoes **dried** by the stove.
                     Mother is **drying** the washing.

duck   *See* **Words for Animals,** page 205.

dust   fine, dry powder in the air, often with bits
dusty   of dirt in it
                     There is **dust** on the table.
                     Mother's hands were **dusty** after she
                cleaned the closet.

each — every
> **Each** child has a desk.

ear — a part of the body through which one hears
> I hear with both my **ears.**

ear — the part of some plants on which the grain grows
> This is an **ear** of corn.

ear′ ly — near the beginning; before the set time
ear′ li er
ear′ li est
> We will leave **early** in the morning.
> I went to school **earlier** than Bob.
> Which of the three buses leaves **earliest**?

earn — to get in return for doing something
> Do you want to **earn** a dime for cleaning the yard?

earth — the planet where we live; the ground
> The **earth** travels around the sun.
> There are many mountains on **earth.**
> We plant seeds in the soft **earth.**

east   a direction; where the sun seems to rise
East is the opposite of *west.*

easy
eas′ i er
eas′ i est

not hard to do or to get
     This trick is **easy** to learn.
     It is an **easier** trick than the other one.
     Joe's trick is the **easiest** one of all.

eat
ate
eat′ en
eat′ ing

to take food through the mouth
     Eat the sandwich and drink your milk.
     The Smiths **ate** at a restaurant.
     Jim has already **eaten** his cake.
     Are you **eating** your lunch?

edge   the outside part of something where it ends
     Each step has a white **edge.**

egg   the first form from which some animals grow; the part of a hen's egg which is used for food
     Birds, turtles, and ants grow from **eggs.**
     Mary Ellen will eat a fried **egg** for breakfast.

ei′ ther   one or the other of the two; each of the two
     You may use **either** red or blue pencils.
     Flowers grow on **either** side of our yard.

elec tric′ i ty   a kind of power which can be used to make light, heat, sound, and motion
    Years ago man learned how to use the **electricity** in nature.

el′ e phant   *See* **Words for Animals,** page 205.

el′ e va tor   a cage or platform which carries people or things up and down to different floors in a building
    Mary went to the third floor in the **elevator.**

else   other; different
    Will somebody **else** play with us?
    What **else** can we do?

emp′ ty   having nothing inside
    Paul finished his milk, and now his glass is **empty.**

end   the last or the finish
    December is at the **end** of the year.

en′ e my   one who is against a person or a thing
en′ e mies   I would rather have a friend than an **enemy.**

en′ gine   a machine that gives power to make things work
    The **engine** in Father's car needs gasoline to work.

en gi neer′   a person who runs or makes engines; a person who plans and builds such things as roads and bridges

    The **engineer** waved to the children from the train.

    The **engineer** planned a new bridge.

en joy′   to have fun with

    Most children **enjoy** playing games.

enough   as much as needed

    I am hungry, because I didn't eat **enough** breakfast.

en′ ve lope   a paper covering in which a letter or anything flat may be mailed

    The address and the stamp are on the **envelope.**

even   flat; about the same; able to be divided by two without a remainder

    The road was **even** instead of bumpy.

    Make the edges of the paper **even.**

    Four and six are **even** numbers.

eve′ ning   the close of the day and the start of night

    We eat supper in the **evening.**

ev′ er   at any time

    Have you **ever** ridden on the subway?

eve′ ry   each one of a group

    Every child made a picture.

eve′ ry thing   each thing; the opposite of *nothing*

Everything for lunch is on the table.

I read **everything** I can about dogs.

ex cite′   to stir up one's feelings
  ex cit′ ing   Parades **excite** many people.

The boys are **exciting** the dog by running around.

ex cite′ ment   an excited condition

The fire at the post office caused a lot of **excitement.**

ex pect′   to plan for

The weatherman said we could **expect** rain today.

ex plain′   to give the meaning of; to tell how

Please **explain** the directions.

I hope the magician will **explain** how he does the trick.

ex plore′   to travel or to go into a place that is
  ex plor′ ing   almost unknown

Astronauts **explore** outer space.

The boys want to **explore** the cave.

The girls were **exploring** the old trunks in the basement.

eye   a part of the body to see with; something like an eye, such as the hole in a needle

I see with both my **eyes.**

The **eye** of the needle is very small.

face
- the front part of the head where the eyes, the nose, and the mouth are; the front or most important side

    You must look in a mirror to see your own **face.**

    There are at least two hands on the **face** of a clock.

fac′ ing
- to have the front toward

    The children **face** the flag and sing.
    The houses are **facing** the street.

fair

honest; clear; not good and not bad

    Miss Smith is **fair** when she corrects papers.

    The weather is **fair** and warm.

    Since the show was only **fair,** I don't want to see it again.

fair

a place where things are shown and sometimes sold

    Mother's cake won a blue ribbon at the **fair.**

    There is a book **fair** at our school.

fairy **fair′ ies**	a make-believe person who does magical things Peggy dressed like a **fairy** for the Halloween party.

fall
  fell
  fall′ en
  fall′ ing

to come down from above
    Leaves **fall** from the maple trees.
    Richard **fell** off his bicycle.
    The temperature has **fallen** fifteen degrees.
    Rain is **falling** now.

fall

the season between summer and winter
    We rake leaves in the **fall.**

fam′ i ly
  fam′ i lies

a father, a mother, and their children
    There are four boys in the Hill **family.**

far
  far′ ther
  far′ thest

a long way
    John lives **far** from school.
    Mike lives **farther** from school than I do.
    Of all the children, Beth lives **farthest** from school.

farm

the land where one raises plants and animals
    Some people drive to the country to get fresh eggs at a **farm.**

farm′ er   one who makes a living on a farm
A good **farmer** must know how to care for the farm.

fast   quick; quickly
Lisa is a **fast** worker.
I can run **fast.**

fat   ● an oily mass, such as found in the bodies of animals and in whole milk
The white part of uncooked bacon is the **fat.**

fat′ ter
fat′ test   ● having a full, round body
The **fat** clown is in the front.
He is **fatter** than the other clowns.
The **fattest** clown makes us laugh.

fa′ ther   the male parent
My mother and my **father** are my parents.

feast   a large, rich meal
On Thanksgiving Day many people have a **feast.**

feath′ er   one of the parts that cover a bird's body
The **feather** is from a bluebird.

feed
fed
feed′ ing   to give food to
We **feed** King dog food.
Who **fed** the baby?
Tina is **feeding** the kittens some milk.

feel
felt
feel′ ing
to know through a sense of touch; to be
Betty could **feel** the cold snowflakes on her cheeks.
Do you **feel** better?
Jack **felt** his way along the dark hall.
I am **feeling** happy today.

feet   *See* **foot.**

fell   *See* **fall.**

felt   *See* **feel.**

fence   a wall, often made of wire or wood, which is put around a field or a yard to keep things in or out
The **fence** keeps the baby inside the yard.

few   at least two, but not many
Only a **few** roses bloomed.

field   an open piece of land which usually has grass or crops growing on it
Corn is growing in the **field.**

fight   ● a contest or a quarrel
The boys had a **fight.**

fought
fight′ ing
● to hit one another; to work against
Little children sometimes **fight** about toys.
The soldiers **fought** their enemies.
The firemen are **fighting** the fire.

fill to make full
> **Fill** the bowl with soup.
> The dentist will **fill** my tooth.

find to look for and to get; to come upon
found
find′ ing
> I must **find** my ticket for the show.
> Jim **found** a dime near school.
> The children are **finding** shells on the beach.

fine thin; very good
> Rope is thick, but thread is **fine.**
> The singer had a **fine** voice.

fine money paid by a person who has done something wrong
> Tom had to pay a **fine** at the library, because he returned his book late.

fin′ ger one of the five parts at the end of the hand
> One **finger** is raised.

fire hot, bright flame caused by something burning
> The **fire** is spreading across the grassy field.

fire′ man one who fights a fire
fire′ men
> The **fireman** will fight the fire.

first   before anything or anyone else
        January is the **first** month of the year.

fish   *See* **Words for Animals**, page 205.
   fish or **fish′ es**

flag   a piece of cloth whose colors and patterns
        are planned to stand for a country; a piece
        of cloth used as a signal
            The American **flag** is red, white, and
        blue.
            A red **flag** on a truck means danger.

flash   a sudden light
   flash′ es   Did you see a **flash** of light?

flat   smooth and even
   flat′ ter   The top of a table is **flat.**
   flat′ test   Some land is **flatter** than other land.
            Give me the **flattest** dish on the shelf.

flew   *See* **fly.**

float   to rest on or to be held up by a liquid or
        by air
            Balloons **float** in the air.

flood   a great overflow, usually of liquid
            Because so much rain fell, there was a
        flood.

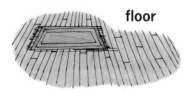

floor
the part on which one walks in a room or in a building
> A rug is on the **floor.**

flour
a powder which is ground from grain, such as wheat, and used in baking
> **Flour** is used in making bread.

flow′ er
the blossom on a plant
> The **flower** on the plant is pink.

fly
flies
flew
flown
fly′ ing
to move through the air
> A bird can **fly** because he has wings.
> The airplane **flies** above the clouds.
> The bee **flew** into the flower.
> Have you **flown** in a helicopter?
> The kites are **flying** high in the sky. .

fly
flies
See **Words for Animals,** page 205.

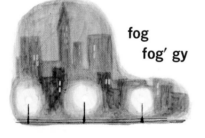

fog
fog′ gy
a cloud of fine drops of water which is low in the sky
> **Fog** is hanging over the city.
> It is a **foggy** night.

fol′ low
to come after; to go along
> November always **follows** October.
> **Follow** this road up the hill.

food   anything that a plant, a person, or an animal eats or drinks to stay alive
    Milk is good **food.**

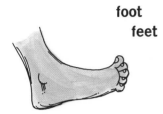

foot
feet   a part of the body on which one stands; the bottom; a measure of length
    My **foot** is at the end of my leg.
    The baby sat at the **foot** of the stairs.
    A **foot** is twelve inches long.

foot′ ball   a game between two teams; the ball that is used in the game
    There are eleven players on each team in **football.**
    A player may kick, throw, or run with the **football.**

for   This present is **for** you.
    The apples are three **for** a quarter.
    Aunt Ann works **for** a large company.

for′ est   very thick woods
    There are many trees in a **forest.**

for get′
  for got′
  for got′ ten
  for get′ ting   not to remember
    If I am in a hurry, I **forget** to do things.
    Chris **forgot** to feed the goldfish.
    Jean has **forgotten** how to knit.
    Karen is always **forgetting** her lunch.

fork   a handle with long points at one end
               which is used to pick up food
                   When I eat, I use a **fork.**

fort   a strong place to protect people from the
               enemy
                   The pioneers built a **fort** where they
               could be safe.

fought   *See* **fight.**

found   *See* **find.**

fox   *See* **Words for Animals,** page 205.
  fox' es or **fox**

fresh   just grown or made; pure; clean
                   The vegetables are **fresh.**
                   The open window lets in **fresh** air.
                   Mother put **fresh** sheets on the bed.

friend   a person you know well and like
                   My **friend** and I like to play together.

fright' en to make afraid
                   Did the storm **frighten** you?

frisky   lively and playful
                   The **frisky** puppy is playing with the
               scarf.

frog   *See* **Words for Animals,** page 205.

from out of; the opposite of *to;* starting with
Who took the flowers **from** this room?
I received a card **from** Al.
Amy comes a week **from** today.

front first; facing forward, not to the back
May I sit in the **front** seat?

fruit the part of a plant which holds the seeds
and which is often good to eat
Apples and oranges are two kinds of
fruit.

full without room for any more
The basket is **full** of apples.

fun a happy, gay time
We had **fun** playing ball.

fun′ ny causing people to laugh
fun′ ni er   I will tell you a **funny** story.
fun′ ni est   Some jokes are **funnier** than others.
Jack wore the **funniest** costume at the
party.

fur the coat of hair that covers many animals
fur′ ry   The coat is made of **fur.**
A kitten's **fur** is soft.
A squirrel is a **furry** animal.

game   a kind of play

    Most children know how to play the **game** hide-and-seek.

ga rage'   a building where cars and trucks are kept; a shop where cars are fixed

    The car is in the **garage.**

    The man at the **garage** fixed the car.

gar' den   a piece of ground where fruits, flowers, and vegetables are grown

    Tomatoes are growing in this **garden.**

gas   something, such as air, which has no shape of its own and which can fill up any amount of space

    The smoke from a burning candle is **gas.**

    Sometimes **gas** is used in stoves.

gas' o line   a liquid which is used to make some engines run

    Father buys **gasoline** for our car.

gate	a door that opens and closes in a wall or a fence

Penny closed the **gate** to keep the dog out of the garden.

gave   *See* **give.**

gen' tle   kind; soft
  gen' tly
Mother gave the baby a **gentle** pat.
A **gentle** breeze lightly blew the leaves.
She speaks **gently.**

ge ra' ni um   *See* **Words for Flowers,** page 196.

get   to receive or to take; to come; to become
  got
  got' ten
  or **got**
  get' ting
I **get** books at the library.
Who **got** here first?
The kittens have **gotten** bigger.
Barbara is **getting** a new coat.

ghost   a bodiless being, sometimes thought to be a person who has died
The story about the **ghost** scared me.

gi' ant   a huge man
In the story the **giant** held the boy inside his large hand.

gi raffe'   *See* **Words for Animals,** page 205.

girl   a female child
That **girl** is my sister.

give
  gave
  giv′ en
  giv′ ing

to let someone or something have
    I will **give** you a penny.
    The man **gave** the fence a coat of paint.
    The teacher has **given** us new pencils.
    Ted is **giving** the dog a bath.

glad

pleased
    The children are **glad** that Paul is not sick anymore.

glass
  glass′ es

something hard which can usually be seen through and which can be easily broken; a drinking cup, usually made of glass
    A window has a large sheet of **glass** set in it.
    I drink milk from a **glass.**

glove

a covering for the hand which usually has a place for each finger
    In chilly weather wool **gloves** keep your hands warm.

go
  goes
  went
  gone
  go′ ing

to move along
    Jim will **go** to school soon.
    The bus **goes** past our house.
    Nancy **went** to the store.
    The Kanes have **gone** to the beach.
    Are you **going** to the library?

goat   *See* **Words for Animals,** page 205.

gold   a bright yellow metal
         Many rings are made of **gold.**

good   pleasing or enjoyable; well-behaved
  bet′ ter   That was a **good** show.
  best   John is a **good** boy.
         I think plums are **better** than pears.
         Tom is my **best** friend.

good-by′
   or   something said when a person leaves
good-bye′   **"Good-by,"** called the girls as they
       left the party.

goose   *See* **Words for Animals,** page 205.
  geese

go ril′ la   *See* **Words for Animals,** page 206.

got   *See* **get.**

grade   one class in school; a mark received for
       work done
         Ted is in the third **grade.**
         Beth got a high **grade** in spelling.

grand′ fa ther   the father of one's father or mother
         My **grandfather** is the oldest
       person in our family.

grand′ moth er   the mother of one's father or mother

I have two **grandmothers.**

grape   *See* **Words for Fruits,** page 198.

grape′ fruit   *See* **Words for Fruits,** page 198.

grass   a plant with thin green shoots, or leaves, which grows on lawns, meadows, and fields

Mr. Jackson cuts the **grass** in the school yard.

grass′ hop per   *See* **Words for Animals,** page 206.

great   big; important

A **great** number of people watched the ball game.

George Washington was a **great** man.

grew   *See* **grow.**

gro′ cer   a person who sells food and some things for the home

Mother buys food every week from the **grocer.**

gro′ cery   the store where food and some things for the home are sold

People shop at the **grocery.**

ground   the soil; the land
         We plant seeds in the **ground.**

group   a number of people or things together
         A **group** of us played baseball.

grow   to become larger
  grew   As I **grow** bigger, my clothes seem
  grown   to be smaller.
  grow' ing   Jill **grew** one inch last year.
         The plant has **grown** quickly.
         Our city is **growing** fast.

growl   a deep, usually angry, sound
         Biff gave a low **growl** at the strange
person.

gruff   being rough in actions, looks, or speech
  gruff' ly   The angry man has a **gruff** voice.
         He speaks **gruffly.**

guess   to try to give an answer when one is not
  guess' es   sure
         Can you **guess** how the story ends?
         Jenny often **guesses** the answers to
riddles.

gun   a weapon which can be made to shoot
something, such as bullets
         The officer wore a **gun** in a holster.

had   *See* **have.**

hail   chunks of frozen rain
     During the storm, **hail** beat noisily against the window.

hair   the fine pieces growing from the skin of people and some animals
     I like to brush my **hair.**

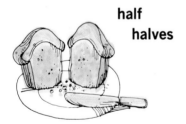

half
halves   one of two equal parts which together make the whole of something
     Ben cut the cupcake in **half.**
     We will go in **half** an hour.

hall   a small room or narrow way in a house or building; a large room or building
     Mary's classroom is at the end of the **hall.**
     Aunt June came in the front door and left her coat in the **hall.**
     The fair was held in a large **hall.**

ham′ burg er ground beef which is often shaped into flat patties before it is cooked
I put my **hamburger** into a bun.

ham′ mer a tool with a handle and a head which is used to drive nails
A builder uses a **hammer.**

ham′ ster *See* **Words for Animals,** page 206.

hand the end part of one's arm; a pointer, such as on a clock
I have five fingers on each **hand.**
There are **hands** on a clock.

hand′ ker chief a soft, often square, piece of cloth which is usually used to wipe the nose and the face
I use a cotton **handkerchief.**

han′ dle • a part of a thing to be held by the hand
You carry a pail by its **handle.**

han′ dling • to touch or to hold with the hand
Handle a sharp knife with care.
The nurse is **handling** the baby gently.

handy useful
A pencil is a **handy** tool.

hang
hung
hang′ ing

to fasten or to be fastened to a rod, a hook, or something above

Dick will **hang** up his clothes.

Tim **hung** the picture on the wall.

Clothes are **hanging** on the line.

hap′ pen

to take place

Many things **happen** each day.

hap′ pi ness

the feeling of gladness; joy

We wished Nancy **happiness** on her birthday.

hap′ py
hap′ pi er
hap′ pi est

glad or pleasant

Danny is a **happy** boy.

I feel **happier** than I did.

This is the **happiest** birthday I have ever had.

hard

firm; not soft; not easy

The candy was so **hard** that I could not break it in half.

Jim had a **hard** time carrying the heavy box.

hard′ ly

not quite; just about

We **hardly** had time to catch the bus.

hat

a covering for the top part of the head

You wear a **hat** on your head.

hatch
hatch′ es
to come out of an egg
    I saw a chick **hatch** from its shell.
    A baby duck **hatches** in about a month.

have
has
had
hav′ ing
to own; to be forced; to hold
    I **have** a new ring.
    Tom **has** to go to bed early.
    Our class **had** a puppet show last week.
    Dick is **having** a birthday soon.

hay
grasses or plants, such as clover, which
are cut and dried and used as food for
some animals
    Horses, cows, and sheep eat **hay.**

he
his
him
the boy, man, or male animal spoken
about
    He is my uncle.
    His name is Mr. Baker.
    I helped **him** clean the basement.
    The truck in the driveway is **his.**

head
the top part of the body; the front;
the top
    The man has hair on his **head.**
    Larry marched at the **head** of the
parade.
    The **head** of a nail is at one end, and
the point is at the other.

hear **heard** **hear′ ing**	to receive sounds through the ear; to learn by listening Can you **hear** Jim whispering? We **heard** the good news. Tim was **hearing** noises in the dark.

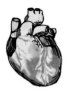

heart — the part of the body inside the chest that pumps the blood and helps to keep the body alive; a ♡ shape
When you run, your **heart** beats faster.
The valentine **heart** is red.

heat — the opposite of *cold*
The sun gives off **heat.**

heavy — hard to lift because of weight
heav′ i er — The **heavy** suitcase was hard to carry.
heav′ i est — This box is **heavier** than yours.
Father carried the **heaviest** box.

held — *See* **hold.**

hel′ i cop′ ter — an aircraft without wings which is lifted and moved by whirling blades on top and often at the back
A **helicopter** is able to fly straight up when it leaves the ground.

hel lo′ — a greeting you say when you first see or talk to someone
"Hello!" said Ann when she met Jill.

help
to be useful to; to do something for
> May I **help** you?
> My eyeglasses **help** me to see.

her
hers
the girl, woman, or female animal spoken about; belonging to her; a form of *she*
> Cathy is my friend, and I like **her.**
> She left **her** doll in the yard.
> The doll bed is **hers,** too.

herd
a number of the same kind of animal, such as cows, that are together
> Cowboys watched the **herd** of cattle.

here
in this place; to this place
> "Put the book **here,** not there," said the teacher.
> **Here** they come!

hi bis′ cus
See **Words for Flowers,** page 196.

hide
hid
hid′ den
or **hid**
hid′ ing
to keep out of sight; to put away
> You **hide,** and we will try to find you.
> Mother **hid** the presents.
> Where have you **hidden** the candy?
> The boys are **hiding** from Allan.

high
tall; above the ground
> The top of the bookcase is too **high** for me to reach.
> Jets fly **high** in the sky.

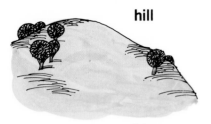

hill	a raised part of the earth which is smaller than a mountain
	The children like to climb to the top of the **hill.**

him	the boy, man, or male animal spoken about; a form of *he*
	I had a race with Ed, and I beat **him.**

hip po pot' a mus   *See* **Words for Animals,** page 206.

his	belonging to him; a form of *he*
his	Jerry is looking for **his** jacket.
	The red jacket is **his.**

hit	to come against with force
hit	The low branch may **hit** your head.
hit' ting	Paul **hit** the ball with a bat.
	The boy is **hitting** his brother.

hold	to take and keep; not to let go
held	Jack will **hold** the package.
hold' ing	Susie **held** the kitten in her lap.
	Who is **holding** the flag?

hole	an open or hollow place
	The puppy dug a **hole** in the garden.
	There is a **hole** in my pocket.

hol' low	empty
	A chipmunk ran into the **hollow** log.

home   a place where one lives
        In the morning I leave **home** and go to school.

hon′ ey   a sweet, yellow liquid made by bees from the liquid of flowers
        Honey is sweet and sticky.

honk   to make a sound like the cry of a wild goose
        Car horns can **honk** loudly.

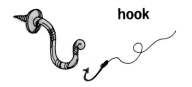

hook   a curved piece of metal or wood for catching or holding something
        There is a **hook** in the closet.
        Janet put a worm on the **hook.**

hope   to wish
hop′ ing   I **hope** you will play with me.
        Many children **hope** to be famous astronauts.
        Mother is **hoping** Susan will come today.

horn   a hard growth on the heads of some animals, such as cattle; something hollow which is blown through to make a sound; a warning signal, as on a car
        A goat has **horns.**
        Tom tooted the **horn** in time to the music.
        Mother honked the **horn** at the dog.

hor′ net   *See* **Words for Animals,** page 206.

horse   *See* **Words for Animals,** page 206.

hos′ pi tal   a place where sick or hurt people or animals are taken care of

      Doctors and nurses work at the **hospital.**

hot
   hot′ ter
   hot′ test   having much heat; having a burning feeling

      A fire is **hot.**
      The sun will make the air **hotter.**
      This is the **hottest** day we have had.

hour   a measure of time

      There are sixty minutes in an **hour.**

house   a building where people live

      A family lives in the **house.**
      The **house** has six rooms.

how   in what way; to what degree

      I don't know **how** to do that.
      How tall is your brother?

howl   to give a long, loud, and often sad cry

      Our dog can **howl** like a wolf.
      Did you hear the wind **howl** during the storm?

hun′ dred   ten times ten; the number for which 100 stands
>   Ninety-nine and one make a **hundred.**
>   One **hundred** pennies equal a dollar.

hung   *See* **hang.**

hun′ gry   feeling the need for food
>   I am always **hungry** before dinner.

hunt   to look for or to chase
>   We will **hunt** for peanuts at my party.
>   Some cats **hunt** mice.

hur′ ri cane   a storm with strong, whirling winds and heavy rain
>   The **hurricane** swept along the coast.

hur′ ry   to move quickly
hur′ ries   >   Some people **hurry** to catch the train.
hur′ ried   >   Sue **hurries** to meet her friends.
hur′ ry ing   >   I slept late, so I **hurried** to school.
>   Mrs. Johnson is **hurrying** to work.

hurt   to cause pain to
hurt   >   You can **hurt** yourself with a knife.
>   Jean **hurt** her knee when she fell.

hus′ band   a married man; a man who has a wife
>   My father is my mother's **husband.**

I   the one who is speaking or writing

me   Mark and **I** play together.

my   He asked **me** to play ball.

mine   That is **my** baseball.

                     The bat is **mine,** too.

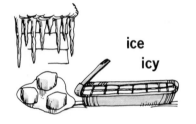

ice   water that has been frozen

icy   When water freezes, it becomes **ice.**

                     In winter some roads are **icy.**

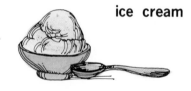

ice cream   a dessert made by mixing and freezing
cream, sugar, eggs, and flavoring

                     Sam likes strawberry **ice cream.**

idea   a plan or a thought

                     Sally has a good **idea** for a story.

if   in case; whether

                     If it snows, we will not go.

                     I wonder **if** they will come.

im por′ tant   chief; of value

                     New York is an **important** city.

                     It is **important** to follow the rules.

in   inside; within; the opposite of *out*
                 Mr. Jones is **in** the bank.
                 They live **in** Michigan.
                 I can be there **in** an hour.

inch   a measure of length
inch′ es   The line is an **inch** long.
                     An **inch** is smaller than a foot.

In′ di an   a member of the native American race; a
                 person from India
                     The **Indian** is weaving a blanket.
                     People in India are called **Indians.**

In′ di an Paint′ brush
                 See **Words for Flowers,** page 196.

in′ sect   a small animal which has three parts to
                 its body, six legs, and sometimes wings
                     A fly is an **insect.**

in′ side   the part within; the opposite of *outside*
                     The **inside** of the house is dark.

in′ to   to the inside of; to a certain condition
                     He is going **into** the house.
                     We ran **into** rain on our way home.

iris   *See* **Words for Flowers,** page 196.
iris es

iron ●a useful metal from which things, such as machines and tools, are made; a tool with a handle and a wide, flat bottom

A fire hydrant is made of **iron.**
Our **iron** uses electricity.

●to take the wrinkles from clothes by using a heated iron

Mother **irons** our clothes.

is a form that is used to show present time (Use with words that mean only one, except the words *I* and *you.*)

It **is** nine o'clock.
Tom **is** glad that he **is** in the play.
The baby **is** crying.

is′ land a piece of land that has water on all sides

We had to take a boat to the **island.**

it the thing, the animal, or the person spoken about

Take the dish, and handle **it** carefully.
The dog chased the squirrel, but he could not catch **it.**

its belonging to the thing or the animal spoken about

I saw a jet and heard **its** roar.
The dog hurt **its** paw.

jack′ et
a short coat
    The boy is wearing a green **jacket.**

jar
a wide-mouthed container, usually made of glass, for holding liquids or solids
    The **jar** was filled with applesauce.

jet
a stream of liquid or gas sent with force
    A **jet** of water came from the fountain.

jet plane
an airplane with an engine which forces out a stream of hot air and gas powerful enough to fly the airplane
    A **jet plane** can fly very fast.

job
work; work for pay
    Washing windows is a hard **job.**
    George has a **job** as a paper boy.

join
to put together; to become a part of
    We **join** hands to make a circle.
    My older brother may **join** a club at school.

joke   something said or done which usually makes people laugh
                    John told a funny **joke.**

jol' ly   full of cheer
  jol' li er   The man is **jolly.**
  jol' li est   He is **jollier** than his wife.
                    He is the **jolliest** person I know.

joy   much happiness
                    Thanksgiving is a time of **joy.**

juice   the liquid part that comes from fruits, vegetables, and meat
  juicy   I like to drink orange **juice.**
                    Some tomatoes are **juicy.**

jump   to leap into the air
                    Sam can **jump** higher than the other boys in his class.

jun' gle   land covered with a thick growth of trees and bushes, especially in the tropics
                    There are often tigers in the **jungle.**

just   exactly; a short time ago; only
                    I have **just** one penny.
                    They have **just** left.
                    The noise is **just** the door rattling.

kan ga roo'   *See* **Words for Animals**, page 206.

keep
  kept
  keep' ing

to have without giving away; to have and to take care of
  May I **keep** the red pencil?
  Andrea **kept** the dime she found.
  Carol is **keeping** Lynn's dog for her.

key

a small piece of metal for opening and closing a lock; one of many parts used for playing a piano or working a typewriter
  Mary turned the **key** in the lock.
  You must push down a typewriter **key**.

kick

to strike with the foot or feet
  He can **kick** the football.
  You **kick** the water when you swim.

kind

being good to others; gentle
  Our teacher is **kind** to us.

kind

type; sort
  What **kind** of fruit do you like?

king
a man who rules a country
　　Sometimes a **king** wears a crown.

kitch' en
a room where food is made ready
　　The stove and the sink are in the **kitchen.**

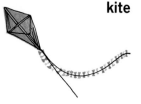

kite
a light wooden frame covered with cloth or paper and flown in the air at the end of a string
　　John put a long tail on his **kite.**

kit' ten
See **Words for Animals,** page 206.

knew
See **know.**

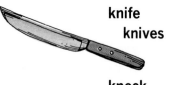

knife
knives
a tool that has a handle and a sharp edge
　　We cut meat with a **knife.**

knock
to hit hard; to bump into and make fall
　　I will **knock** on the door.
　　Did you **knock** the lamp over?

know
knew
known
know' ing
to be sure; to be familiar with
　　You **know** how to spell many words.
　　He **knew** Mary before he met Joan.
　　Alice has **known** that song for years.
　　Keep him from **knowing** the secret.

kum' quat
See **Words for Fruits,** page 199.

lad

a boy
> The **lad** grew to be a strong man.

lad′ der

a set of steps which are fastened into two long pieces of wood or metal and which can usually be moved from place to place
> The man used a **ladder** to reach the roof.

la′ dy
la′ dies

a woman
> Miss Brooks is a young **lady.**

la′ dy bug

See **Words for Animals,** page 206.

lake

a body of water surrounded by land
> We sailed in a boat around the **lake.**
> A **lake** is often larger than a pond.

lamb

See **Words for Animals,** page 207.

lame

having a hurt leg; not able to walk well
> The **lame** dog has a sore paw.
> Jack was **lame** after he fell.

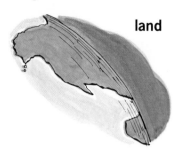

land

● the hard part of the earth's surface; ground; a country

Earth is covered with **land** and water.

Most cities have **land** set aside for parks.

America is our **land.**

● to bring down to earth

Pilots **land** the planes on a runway.

large

very big; great

An elephant is very **large.**

last

after all the rest

The little boy is the **last** person in line.

I ate the **last** plum.

last

to continue; to go on

The show will **last** an hour.

We must water the flowers so that they will **last** longer.

late

after the usual time; the opposite of *early*

Hurry, or you will be **late** for dinner.

late' ly

not long ago; a little while ago

Have you read a book **lately**?

Lately we added to our library.

laugh

to make happy sounds to show that you have seen or heard something funny

People **laugh** at funny stories.

lay
laid
lay′ ing

to put down; to put in place
    Jill will **lay** the book on the table.
    Ellen **laid** the blanket on the bed.
    The workman is **laying** the bricks.

la′ zy
la′ zi er
la′ zi est

not very willing to work
    Alice was too **lazy** to clean her room.
    Herb is **lazier** than his brother.
    Sally is the **laziest** girl I know.

lead
led
lead′ ing

to go first, often to show the way
    The boy **leads** the pony.
    A pretty girl **led** the parade.
    Jack was **leading** in the race.

lead′ er

one who shows the way or leads
    Mr. Long is the **leader** of the band.

leaf
leaves

a thin, flat, and usually green part that
grows on plants and trees
    A **leaf** blew down from the tree.

learn

to find out; to come to know
    Children **learn** many things in school.
    We will **learn** that poem.

leath′ er

the skin of certain animals that has been
tanned, or treated in a special way
    An alligator's skin is often used to
make **leather.**

leave   to go away; to let stay behind; to let stay
  left   a certain way
  leav' ing
> Henry will **leave** on the early bus.
> Jack **left** his coat at school.
> Betty is **leaving** the door open.

left   a direction; the opposite of *right*
> The boy is raising his **left** arm.
> The bus made a **left** turn.

leg   a part of the body on which people and animals stand or walk; anything used like a leg
> A person has two **legs.**
> Most tables have four **legs.**

lem' on   See **Words for Fruits,** page 199.

lem on ade' a drink made from the juice of lemons, sugar, and water
> **Lemonade** with ice tastes good.

leop' ard   See **Words for Animals,** page 207.

less   smaller in amount; not so much
> Pat spent **less** than a dollar.

let   to allow
  let
  let' ting
> I will **let** you ride my bicycle.
> Last week Jan **let** Beth use her pen.
> Father is **letting** Sport ride in the car.

let′ ter   one of the written or printed signs or marks which are used to stand for sounds in words; a written message

> The last **letter** in our alphabet is *z*.
> He mailed the **letter**.

let′ tuce   *See* **Words for Vegetables,** page 201.

li′ brary
li′ brar ies   a place where books are kept; a large group of books

> Mary got her book at the **library.**
> We have books about space in our classroom **library.**

lie   an untrue statement or story which is told to cheat or mislead

> It is not right to tell a **lie.**

lie
lay
lain
ly′ ing   to have the body out flat; to be flat

> Ron likes to **lie** on the beach.
> The bike **lay** on the ground.
> Mother has **lain** on the bed for a nap.
> The sign is **lying** on its side.

life
lives   the condition of being alive; the time in which people, animals, and plants are alive

> A stone has no **life.**
> Grandfather has lived here all his **life.**

lift   to raise or to pick up
> You should **lift** a baby carefully.

light   easy to lift; the opposite of *heavy;* gentle; pale
> This box is **light.**
> There was a **light** tap on the door.
> On clear days the sky is **light** blue.

light   what helps us to see; brightness
> You should have good **light** when you read.
> The sun gives us **light.**

like   almost the same as
> The rumble of the heavy truck sounded **like** thunder.

like   to be pleased with; to enjoy
> Do you think Jim will **like** our present?

line   a long rope or string; a row; a long mark
> Mother hung a towel on the **line.**
> The children are standing in **line.**
> John wrote his name on the top **line.**

line
lin' ing   to put paper or cloth along the inside of something, such as a box or a coat
> The girls will **line** the box with paper.
> Mother is **lining** my coat.

li′ on   *See* **Words for Animals,** page 207.

liq′ uid   something, such as water, that flows
                   easily; not a solid or a gas
                      Milk is a **liquid.**

lis′ ten   to try to hear; to pay attention to by
                   hearing
                      I often **listen** to the radio.

lit′ tle   small; not big; not much
                      My **little** sister is learning to read.
                      I poured a **little** water on the plant.

live   to be alive; to make your home
    liv′ ing   You may **live** to be ninety years old.
                      On which street do you **live**?
                      The Smiths are now **living** in Texas.

live′ ly   full of life; frisky
                      The **lively** dogs chased one another.

liz′ ard   *See* **Words for Animals,** page 207.

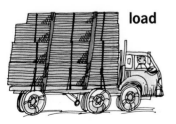

load   • the things being carried
                      The truck carries a **load** of lumber.

                   • to put in something to be carried
                      The men will **load** the moving van.

lob′ ster   *See* **Words for Animals,** page 207.

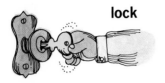

lock   to fasten something, such as a door, so that it will not open

You can **lock** the door with the key.

Father **locks** the trunk of the car.

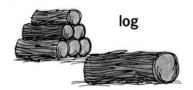

log   a piece of wood as it comes from a tree

I'll put another **log** in the fireplace.

long   taking much time; having a great measure from one end to another; the opposite of *short*

Miss Lane read to us for a **long** time.

Ted found a **long** rope.

look   to try to see; to pay attention to by seeing

Look both ways before you cross the street.

You should **look** at the person who is giving a report in class.

loose   not tied; not tight enough

Jill tied the dog to the fence, but he got **loose.**

My shoes are too **loose.**

lose   not to be able to find; to have missing; not to win
lost
los′ ing   If you don't keep your ticket in a safe place, you may **lose** it.

My little brother **lost** his first tooth.

The girls are **losing** the race.

lot
a piece of land or ground; a great number
We play ball in the empty **lot.**
There are a **lot** of books in the library.

loud
loud′ ly
having a great sound; not quiet; very noisy
Thunder makes a **loud** sound.
The boys called **loudly.**

love
to have a close feeling for
I **love** my parents.

love′ ly
beautiful; very pleasing
The golden sunset was **lovely.**

low
near the ground or the bottom; not high
The girl put her doll on a **low** chair.
Tim has a **low** voice.

low′ er
to let down
We **lower** the window shades at night.

luck
something good or bad which seems to
happen by chance
They had good **luck** fishing.
I had bad **luck** when I broke my leg.

lunch
lunch′ es
a light meal, usually eaten in the middle
of the day
Many children eat **lunch** at school.

ma chine′   a thing made up of parts for doing work
      Mother sews faster on a sewing
machine than she does by hand.

made   *See* **make.**

mag′ ic   something supposedly done by a secret
charm
      In the story the witch used **magic** to
turn the prince into a frog.

ma gi′ cian   one who does tricks, as if by magic
      The **magician** can do many tricks.

maid   a woman helper; a young girl
      Mrs. Palmer has a **maid** to help her.
      In a poem a girl is sometimes called
a **maid.**

mail   letters, packages, magazines, and other
things sent through the post office
      The **mail** was left in the mailbox.

make   to build; to put together; to cause to be
  made   Our friends will **make** a tree hut.
  mak′ ing   The baker **made** some good bread
today.
              The sun is **making** the sidewalk hot.

man   a grown-up boy
  men   My father is a **man.**

many   a great number of
         There are **many** feet in a mile.

mar′ ble   a kind of hard rock which takes a beautiful
polish; a small hard ball used in games
         Some buildings are made of **marble.**
         A red **marble** rolled off the table.

march   to walk like a soldier by keeping in step
  march′ es with others
         The boys will **march** in the parade.
         Betty **marches** with the band.

mar′ i gold *See* **Words for Flowers,** page 197.

mark   a line or a dot; a sign; a grade
         Ellen made a **mark** with her crayon.
         A period is a punctuation **mark.**
         Janet received a good **mark** on her
paper.

mar′ ket   a place where things are bought and sold
       Ellen bought some apples and pears at the **market.**

mat′ ter   the trouble
       What is the **matter** with the boy who is crying?

may
   might   to be allowed; to be possible
       May I have a cookie?
       If we don't hurry, we **may** be late.
       Mother told me I **might** go.

may′ be   possibly; perhaps
       Maybe it will rain.

me   the person speaking; a form of *I*
       Bill gave Tom and **me** some candy.

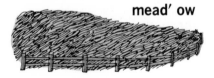

mead′ ow   a grassy field
       The grass in the **meadow** will be cut and dried for hay.

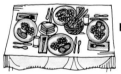

meal   food which is prepared and eaten
       The evening **meal** is on the table.

meal   grain which has been ground
       Some corn is ground into **meal.**

mean   to have as its thought; to have in mind
  meant   I don't know what the words **mean**.
  mean' ing   Tom didn't know what the teacher **meant**.
                  Ann has been **meaning** to write you.

mean   unkind
                  It is **mean** to make fun of someone.

meas' ure   an amount or a size
                  An inch is a **measure** of length.

meat   the flesh of animals which is used for food
                  We buy **meat** at the store.
                  Mother cooked the **meat** for dinner.

meet   to join; to get together; to be introduced to
  met   The children **meet** each other on the
  meet' ing   way to school.
                  The boys **met** on the playground.
                  Joanne's mother is **meeting** the new teacher.

meet' ing   a group of people who come together for some reason
                  Mother has gone to a **meeting** of parents and teachers.
                  The science club had a **meeting**.

men   *See* **man.**

mer' ry   full of fun; gay
  mer' ri er   What a **merry** time we had!
  mer' ri est   This was a **merrier** party than the last one.

         Everyone had the **merriest** time at the circus.

mes' sage   information sent from one person to another

         Ann took a **message** for her father over the telephone.

         We sent a telegraph **message.**

met   *See* **meet.**

mice   *See* **mouse.**

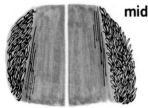

mid' dle   a point halfway between the ends or the sides

         The white line is in the **middle** of the road.

might   *See* **may.**

might   strength; great power
  mighty   Beth swam with all her **might.**
         The giant was a **mighty** man.

mile   a measure of distance
         A **mile** is many times longer than a foot or a yard.

milk
a white liquid which comes from cows and some other mother animals and which is used as food

Milk is a food which helps to make you healthy.

mind
the part of a person which thinks, feels, chooses, and decides

Terry has a good **mind.**

min′ ute
a measure of time; a short time

There are sixty seconds in a **minute** and sixty minutes in an hour.

I'll be ready in a **minute.**

miss
miss′ es
not to catch, to hit, or to get; to feel sad when away from someone or something

You may **miss** the bus if you sleep late.

Did the catcher **miss** the ball?

Grandmother **misses** the children after she leaves them.

Miss
a title given to a girl or a woman who is not married

Miss Smith is getting married.

mit′ ten
a covering for the hand which has one place for the thumb and another place for the other fingers

The **mitten** is made of wool yarn.

mon′ ey   coins and paper bills which are used to pay for things
    The United States government makes the **money** which we use.

mon′ key   *See* **Words for Animals,** page 207.

month   one of the twelve periods of time which together make a year
    December is the last **month** of the year.

moon   a body in the sky that moves around the earth about once a month
    There is a full **moon** tonight.

more   greater in number; additional
    Three books are **more** than two books.
    Do you want **more** potatoes?

morn′ ing   the first part of the day; the time between midnight and noon
    Morning comes before afternoon.

mos qui′ to   *See* **Words for Animals,** page 207.
mos qui′ toes

most   greatest number of; almost all
    William was the winner because he had the **most** votes.
    Most people like to read.

moth' er the female parent

A **mother** takes care of her children.
I help **Mother** by watching the baby.

mo' tor the part that makes a machine go; an engine

A car has a **motor.**

moun' tain a very high hill

A **mountain** may have snow at its top all year round.

mouse *See* **Words for Animals,** page 207.
mice

mouth the opening in the face for taking in food; an opening

When you talk, you must open and close your **mouth.**
Bushes hid the **mouth** of the cave.

move to change from one position or place to
mov' ing another

The men must **move** the furniture.
I can **move** each finger on my hand.
Our neighbors are **moving** to a different city.

Mr. a title for a man; the abbreviation for the word *Mister*

Mr. Jones is Kathy's father.

Mrs. a title for a woman who is married; an abbreviation for the word *Mistress*
Mrs. Hall is Mr. Hall's wife.

much a great amount of; greatly
There was **much** excitement at the Halloween party.
I am **much** taller than I was last year.

mud earth which is wet and sticky
mud′ dy The little girl played in the **mud.**
Her shoes are **muddy.**

mu′ sic the art of putting sounds together in some kind of order
Music can be sung or played on an instrument.

mu si′ cian a person who sings or plays a musical instrument with great skill
The man who played the piano is a fine **musician.**

must have to
We **must** go now, or we will be late.
All people **must** have water to drink.

my belonging to me; a form of *I*
mine **My** book is on the table.
The book on the table is **mine.**

nail   a thin piece of metal, pointed at one end and flat at the other; the hard covering at the end of a finger or a toe

     The carpenter used a hammer to drive the **nail** into the wood.

     I cut the **nail** on my thumb.

name   the special word or words used to stand for a person, an animal, or a thing; a title

     When a baby is born, he is given a **name** by his parents.

     My friend's **name** is Mary Ann Brown.

     What is the **name** of the game you are playing?

near
  near′ ly   not far from; close to

     They live **near** Los Angeles but far from Boston.

     It is **nearly** time for bed.

neck   the part of the body between the head and the shoulders

     A necklace is around the girl's **neck**.

     A giraffe has a long **neck**.

need   must have; should have
                  People **need** food to live.
                  You **need** a coat in cold weather.

neigh′ bor   a person who lives in the next house or in
                  a nearby house
                  We share a garage with our **neighbor.**

nest   a place built by birds for their eggs; a
                  place built by some animals and insects
                  A bird often uses string, twigs, and
                  grass to build his **nest.**
                  Wasps built a **nest** under the roof.

nev′ er   at no time
                  You should **never** play with matches.

new   not used; not known before
                  That shiny bicycle is **new.**
                  I have a **new** friend.

news   story of something that has just happened
                  Mike told us the **news** about the fire.
                  Father watches the **news** on television.

news′ pa per printed sheets of paper which report
                  the happenings of the day and other
                  things of interest to people
                  The **newspaper** has reports of what is
                  happening around the world.

next   nearest; following at once
        Frank is sitting **next** to the window.
        What can we do **next**?

nice   pleasing
nice′ ly   Joan is a **nice** person.
        She sings **nicely.**

nick′ el   a piece of money equal to five cents
        You can buy a candy bar for a **nickel.**

night   the time between evening and morning
        I like to watch the moon and the stars
at **night.**

no   the opposite of *yes;* not any
        No, *i* is not before *a* in *rain.*
        A snake has **no** legs.

noise   a sound, usually not pleasant
nois′ i ly   The gun made a loud **noise.**
noisy   Some children shouted **noisily.**
        The old car's engine is **noisy.**

noon   the middle of the day
        We eat lunch at **noon.**

north   a direction
        North is the opposite of *south.*
        Canada is **north** of the United States.

nose   a part of the face above the mouth
              A person breathes and smells with his
nose.

not   a word which is like *no*
              The land is dry, because we have **not**
had rain.
              There is **not** an *e* in the word *saw.*

note   a short written message; a sign in music
to stand for a sound
              Mother wrote a **note** to tell us where
she was going.
              I try not to miss a **note** when I play
the piano.

noth' ing   not a thing
              The box is empty, because there is
nothing in it.

now   at this time
              Do your work **now,** not later.

num' ber   a word or a sign that tells how many; a
certain amount of
              Two is a **number.**
              A **number** of boys went swimming.

nut   a dry fruit or seed with a hard shell
              Many kinds of **nuts** are good to eat.
              The squirrel nibbled at a **nut.**

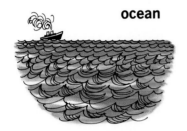

ocean
the body of salt water that covers a great part of the earth; one of the large parts of this main body of water
Ships travel across the **ocean.**
The Atlantic **Ocean** is east of the United States.

o'clock
an abbreviation for *of the clock*
It is nine **o'clock.**

oc' to pus
oc' to pus es
See **Words for Animals,** page 207.

of
belonging to; made from; from; that is
Sandy cleared the top **of** the desk.
The girl held a bunch **of** flowers.
Do you want a piece **of** the pie?
I live in the state **of** Vermont.

off
away from; not on
The wind blew the man's hat **off** his head.
The water has been turned **off.**

of′ ten　　　many times
　　　　　　　　In the summer we **often** go to the
　　　　　　beach.

oh　　　　　a word to express surprise, joy, or other
　　　　　　strong feelings
　　　　　　　　Oh, I broke my glasses!

okra　　　*See* **Words for Vegetables,** page 201.

old　　　　the opposite of *young;* of age; used or
　　　　　　worn; the opposite of *new*
　　　　　　　　The man is **old,** but the boy is young.
　　　　　　　　Martha is eight years **old.**
　　　　　　　　Jan wears **old** clothes when she paints.

on　　　　over and touching; upon; at the time of
　　　　　　　　The clown has a hat **on** her head.
　　　　　　　　There is a picture **on** the wall.
　　　　　　　　We left **on** Monday.

once　　　one time
　　　　　　　　Please read the story **once** more.

on′ ion　　*See* **Words for Vegetables,** page 201.

on′ ly　　　no more than one; just
　　　　　　　　She is my **only** sister.
　　　　　　　　I have **only** two dimes.

open
- fixed so that a person or a thing can go in or out; not closed
  The door is **open.**
  A bee flew through the **open** window.

- to move whatever is keeping a thing closed
  You **open** and close your eyes.

opos' sum   *See* **Words for Animals,** page 208.

op' po site   something which is in no way the same; the very different thing
  Up is the **opposite** of *down.*

or   a word used between words or groups of words that offer a choice
  Are you going by train **or** by bus?

or' ange   *See* **Words for Fruits,** page 199.

or' chard   the ground where fruit trees are grown
  Many apple trees are growing in this **orchard.**

or' chid   *See* **Words for Flowers,** page 197.

oth' er   different from the one just spoken about
  I live on one side of the street, and Patty lives on the **other** side.

our   belonging to us; a form of *we*
  ours
              Our house is on a hill.
              The garage next to the house is also **ours.**

out   away from the inside; the opposite of *in;* at an end
              Mark is going **out** the door.
              Judy looked **out** the window.
              The fire is **out.**

out doors'   in the open air
              Today it is cooler **outdoors** than it is in the house.

out' side'   the outer part; the opposite of *inside*
              The **outside** of the box is blue.

over   above; across; to the other side
              A jet is flying **over** the city.
              Mother laid the blanket **over** the bed.
              The baby learned how to turn **over.**

own

- belonging to oneself
  Mary has her **own** bedroom.

- to have
  Do you **own** a bike?

pack

to put things together in a box or in a suitcase

I will help you **pack** your bag.

We **pack** our clothes before we go on a trip.

pack′ age

a bundle; things packed together

A **package** came in the mail.

Paul bought a **package** of gum.

paid

See **pay.**

pail

a round container with a handle for carrying things; a bucket

Andy carried the **pail** of water.

paint

● solid color mixed with a liquid which dries after it has been spread on something

I used a brush to spread the **paint.**

● to cover with color; to make a picture with paints

Frank will **paint** the garage green.

Many artists **paint.**

pair   two parts or things that go together
Mary has a **pair** of red shoes.

pal′ ace   a large, fine house where a king and a queen might live
The **palace** has beautiful gardens and trees around it.

pan   a wide and not too deep dish, usually made of metal
The bread is baking in a **pan.**

pan′ sy   *See* **Words for Flowers,** page 197.
pan′ sies

pa′ per   something to write on, to wrap things with, and to make things from
We use a lot of **paper** in school.

pa rade′   a group of people marching
A band is leading the Fourth of July **parade.**

park   • land set aside to be used for picnics and fun
There are benches in the city **park.**

• to leave a car for a while
Mother will **park** near the post office.

part   a piece that is less than the whole
You may have **part** of my apple.

par′ ty
par′ ties   a group of people having fun together
The children are having fun at the birthday **party.**

pass
pass′ es   to go by
I **pass** the fire station on my way to school.
The bus **passes** our house.

past   gone by
In the spring winter is **past.**
It is **past** three o'clock.

paste   something, such as flour and water, used to stick pieces of paper together
Betty spread **paste** on the back of the picture before she stuck it in her folder.

pas′ ture   a grassy field where cattle, horses, sheep, and other animals feed
Cattle graze in the **pasture.**

path   a trail which has been made by people or animals walking
We followed the **path** up the hill.

paw   the foot of an animal which has claws
                 A dog has four **paws.**

pay   to give money for things bought or for
  paid   work done
  pay′ ing   Pat will **pay** the paper girl.
                 I **paid** twenty-five cents for a picture
                 of a beautiful horse.
                     Mother is **paying** a bill at the store.

peach   See **Words for Fruits**, page 199.
  peach′ es

pear   See **Words for Fruits**, page 199.

peas   See **Words for Vegetables**, page 201.

peep   to look through a small hole or a crack
                     Joan tried to **peep** through the crack
                 in the high fence.

peep   the small cry of a bird or a chick
                     Baby chickens **peep.**

pen   a tool used for writing with ink
                     I like to write with a **pen.**

pen   a closed yard for animals
                     A farmer often keeps chickens in
                 a **pen.**

pen′ cil   a tool to write or to draw with
I sharpened the point on my **pencil.**

pen′ guin   *See* **Words for Animals,** page 208.

pen′ ny   a one-cent coin
pen′ nies   Bonnie paid a **penny** for a piece of
candy.

peo′ ple   human beings; men, women, and children
People around the world use different
languages.
Many **people** are waiting for the bus.

pep′ per   *See* **Words for Vegetables,** page 201.

pet   an animal which is tamed and treated with
love
My **pet** is a rabbit.

pe tu′ nia   *See* **Words for Flowers,** page 197.

pick   to choose; to take, as from a plant
Kevin will **pick** the next story.
May we **pick** some blueberries?

pic′ nic   an outing to which people bring food to
eat in the open air
The children fixed a basket of food to
take on the **picnic.**

pic′ ture   a drawing; a painting; a photograph
        Beth drew a **picture** with crayons.
        At school there is a **picture** of George Washington.
        Dick has used his camera to take a **picture.**

pie   a pastry which is filled with something, such as fruit or meat, and baked
        Mother made a cherry **pie.**

piece   a part; a bit
        A **piece** of the puzzle is missing.
        May I have a **piece** of candy?
        Jerry found a **piece** of chalk.

pig   See **Words for Animals,** page 208.

pile   many things heaped together
        There is a **pile** of coats on the bed.
        Miss Hill put the papers in a **pile.**

pi′ lot   one who steers a plane or a ship
        The **pilot** landed the airplane on the runway.
        The **pilot** steered the steamboat.

pine′ ap ple   See **Words for Fruits,** page 199.

pipe   a tube through which something, such as water or gas, can flow; a tube of wood, clay, or metal with a bowl at one end which is filled with tobacco

A water **pipe** is fastened under the sink.

That man smokes a **pipe.**

place   • a certain spot; a city, town, state, or country

My bookmark marks the **place** where I stopped reading.

What **places** did you see on your trip?

plac′ ing   • to put or to set in a certain spot

You may **place** the dishes here.

She is **placing** the flowers in a vase.

plan′ et   a heavenly body that moves around the sun

Our earth is a **planet.**

plant   • a living thing, such as a tree, a vegetable, or a flower; any living thing that is not an animal

A tree is a large **plant.**

Most **plants** have roots, stems, and leaves.

• to put seeds or the roots of a plant into the ground

We **plant** seeds in flowerpots.

plate a dish, almost flat and usually round, on which food is served; a flat marker used as home base in baseball

> I put my lunch on a **plate.**
> The batter stands at home **plate.**

play to have fun; to take part in; to make music with

> The children **play** in the yard.
> The girls **play** baseball after school.
> Ann can **play** the piano.

pleas′ ant pleasing
pleas′ ant ly The **pleasant** grocer talked with the people in his store.

> A breeze is **pleasant** on a hot day.
> The girl spoke **pleasantly.**

please ● a polite word you use when you ask for something

> **Please** help me.

● to make glad

> We **please** our teacher when we work.

plum *See* **Words for Fruits,** page 199.

pock′ et a small bag which is sewed in clothing for carrying small things

> Sandra put a handkerchief in her **pocket.**

poin set′ tia *See* **Words for Flowers,** page 197.

point
- a sharp end
  The pencil has a fine **point.**

- to show a place or a direction, often by means of the finger
  Ted will **point** to the correct answer on the chalkboard.

pole
a long, slender, and often rounded piece of wood or metal
  The worker is climbing the telephone **pole.**

po lice′ man
po lice′ men
one whose job it is to keep order in a city, town, or state by seeing that people obey the laws
  A **policeman** helped the lost children find their home.

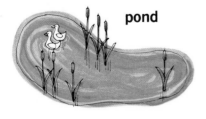

pond
a body of water which is smaller than a lake
  We watched some ducks swimming in the **pond.**

po′ ny
po′ nies
See **Words for Animals,** page 208.

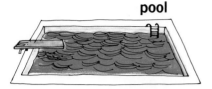

pool a tank of water to swim in; a small pond
There are often swimming races at the **pool.**

poor having few things or little money;
poor' ly needing to be made better
After I lost my money, I was **poor.**
Corn will not grow in **poor** soil.
My cousin writes **poorly.**

pop to break or to open with a short, quick
popped sound
pop' ping The balloon will **pop** if you stick a pin in it.
The popcorn **popped** in the hot pan.
Firecrackers were **popping.**

pop' py See **Words for Flowers,** page 197.
pop' pies

post a piece of wood or iron set in the ground
to support something
A sign is nailed to the **post.**

post' man one whose job it is to deliver and to pick
post' men up letters and packages that are sent
through the mail
The **postman** left two letters in our mailbox.

pot   a deep, often heavy dish which is used to hold food or plants
                   A **pot** of soup is on the stove.

po ta′ to   See **Words for Vegetables,** page 201.
  po ta′ toes

pound   to strike hard
                   Can you feel your heart **pound**?

pound   a measure of weight
                   There are sixteen ounces in a **pound.**

pour   to cause to flow in a steady stream; to flow in a steady stream
                   I'll **pour** the water into the glasses.
                   During a storm the rain sometimes **pours** out of the sky.

pres′ ent   here; now
                   All of the children are **present.**
                   At **present** you are reading a page in a dictionary.

pres′ ent   a gift; something given
                   I made a **present** for my mother.

pres′ i dent   the leader or the person in the highest office of a club or a nation
                   We elected Max **president** of our club.

pret′ ty   pleasing to see or to hear
  pret′ ti er   Mother's blue suit is **pretty.**
  pret′ ti est   Do you think a rose is **prettier** than a
dandelion?
      That is the **prettiest** song I know.

price   the amount of money for which a thing
is bought or sold
      The **price** of the shirt is two dollars.

prince   the son of a king or a queen
      The queen's son is a **prince.**

prin′ cess   the daughter of a king or a queen
      The queen's daughter is a **princess.**

prize   something given for being the best in a
race or a contest
      A **prize** was given to the winner.

proud   thinking well of oneself or of others
  proud′ ly   Ann felt **proud** when she won the prize.
      Mother said, "I am **proud** of you."
      Father smiled **proudly.**

pud′ dle   a small pool of water which is often dirty
      After it rained, there was a big
puddle by the sidewalk.

pull to move towards oneself with force; to tug
 If you **pull** the handle, the wagon will move after you.
 I **pull** my boots on over my shoes.
 The baby likes to **pull** my hair.

pump' kin *See* **Words for Vegetables,** page 201.

pup' pet a small figure of a person or an animal which is moved by wires or the hands
 The **puppet** moves if someone pulls the strings.
 Janet made a hand **puppet.**

pup' py *See* **Words for Animals,** page 208.
pup' pies

push to press against something to move it
push' es away from you
 People are trying to **push** the car out of the snowdrift.
 The little tug **pushes** the boat.

put to place or to lay in a certain place
put   The girls will **put** their coats on.
put' ting I **put** my toys away before I went to bed.
 Mother is **putting** the car in the garage.

quack
to make the sound of a duck
Ducks **quack** noisily.

quar' rel
to argue; to talk angrily
Marcia and June may **quarrel** about which game to play.
I saw a baseball player **quarrel** with the umpire.

quart
a measure
Mother buys milk by the **quart.**
A **quart** is one quarter of a gallon.

quar' ter
a part equal to one-fourth of the whole; a piece of money equal to twenty-five cents, or one-fourth of a dollar
I ate a **quarter** of the orange.
Two dimes and a nickel are the same amount of money as a **quarter.**
A **quarter** is less than a half-dollar.

queen
a woman ruler; the wife of the king
The **queen** lives in a palace.
The people cheered their **queen.**

queer　　odd; strange

　　　　　　The book is about a **queer** little elf.

　　　　　　Jim had a **queer** look on his face after tasting the lemon.

ques' tion　a sentence which is asked when one is trying to find an answer

　　　　　　Bill answered every **question** on the test.

　　　　　　I want to ask a **question.**

quick　　fast

　quick' ly　　The trip to the city was **quick.**

　　　　　　Come **quickly,** or we will be late.

qui' et　　without noise; very still; the opposite of

　qui' et ly　*loud*

　　　　　　The house is **quiet** when everyone is asleep.

　　　　　　The baby played **quietly.**

quilt　　A bedcover, usually made of two pieces of cloth sewed together with a soft lining between them

　　　　　　Grandmother made a pretty **quilt** for my bed.

quite　　really; completely or fully

　　　　　　It is **quite** cold today.

　　　　　　The paint is sticky, because it is not **quite** dry.

rab′ bit   *See* **Words for Animals,** page 208.

rac coon′   *See* **Words for Animals,** page 208.

race   to run to try to beat; to go fast
  rac′ ing   I will **race** you to the tree.
                      Fire engines **race** to a fire.
                      How many sailboats are **racing**?

ra′ dio   a way of sending and receiving sounds
by electrical waves without the use of
connecting wires; the set which receives
radio waves and gives out the sounds
        People get news by **radio.**

        We have a small white **radio** in our
kitchen.

rain   drops of water falling from the clouds
  rainy   People carry umbrellas to keep from
getting wet in the **rain.**
        Rain helps plants to grow.
        There are often dark clouds on **rainy**
days.

raise
rais′ ing

to lift; to put up; to make grow

We **raise** our hands to talk in class.

The custodian **raises** the flag in front of our school.

Some farmers **raise** vegetables.

The wind is **raising** a lot of dust.

rake

● a tool which has a long handle with a row of teeth at one end for moving dirt, grass, or leaves

Jack was using a **rake.**

rak′ ing

● to gather or to smooth with a rake

We **rake** leaves in the fall.

The boy is **raking** the garden.

ran   *See* **run.**

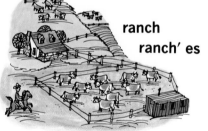

ranch
ranch′ es

a large farm where animals, such as cattle, sheep, and horses, are raised

There are many cattle being raised on this **ranch.**

rang   *See* **ring.**

rasp′ ber ry   *See* **Words for Fruits,** page 199.
rasp′ ber ries

rat   *See* **Words for Animals,** page 208.

rat' tle   to make many short, sharp sounds
   rat' tling   When you shake the tin bank, the
pennies **rattle.**
     The wind is **rattling** the windows.

reach   to touch; to get to; to stretch
   reach' es   Susan can **reach** the top shelf.
     How long does it take you to **reach**
school?
     My arm **reaches** above Aunt Betty's
head.

read   to get the meaning of letters, words, and
   read   signs which are written or printed; to say
   read' ing   aloud what is written or printed
     I like to **read** sports stories.
     Jean has **read** the thermometer.
     Miss Ames is **reading** a letter to the
children.

ready   prepared
     We cannot eat until dinner is **ready.**

real   true
     Is the story **real** or make-believe?

re' al ly   truly
     She is **really** a girl, not a witch.
     The moon seems small, but it is **really**
very large.

re mem′ ber to keep in mind; to be able to think of
again
Can you **remember** the answer?
I wish I could **remember** her name.

rhi noc′ er os *See* **Words for Animals,** page 208.

rich   having much of something
The **rich** king had much gold.
Cream has a **rich** taste.
Plants grow well in **rich** soil.

rid′ dle   a question or a problem that is puzzling
Can you guess the answer to the
riddle?

ride   to be carried on or in something that
rode   moves, such as a horse or a car
rid′ den   Cowboys **ride** horseback.
rid′ ing   We **rode** our bicycles to school.
Have you ever **ridden** a camel?
Carol is **riding** in the back seat.

right   a direction; the opposite of *left;* good;
correct; the opposite of *wrong*
Tim is writing with his **right** hand.
We made a **right** turn at the corner.
It is **right** to be kind and honest.
Did you have the **right** answer?

ring   a circle of metal which sometimes has a stone set in it; a circle

    Mother wears a **ring** on her finger.

    Horses walked into the circus **ring.**

    The children held hands and stood in a **ring** to play the game.

ring   to make a clear sound, such as with a bell
rang
rung
ring′ ing

    Telephones **ring.**

    Ted **rang** the bell on his bicycle.

    Has the school bell **rung**?

    The doorbell is **ringing.**

riv′ er   a large, flowing stream of water

    The **river** flows into the ocean.

    The bridge crosses the **river.**

road   a long, open way to travel on

    There are many cars on the **road.**

    A dirt **road** leads to the beach.

roar   to make a loud noise

    Lions **roar.**

rock   a hard mass found in the ground

    The hard part of the earth's surface is **rock.**

    Terry found a big **rock** on the lawn.

rock
to move backward and forward or sideways

> You can **rock** in this kind of chair.
> The waves **rock** the boat.

rode
See **ride.**

ro' deo
a contest of skill in such things as roping cattle and riding horses

> Cowboys rode horses at the **rodeo.**

roll
• a kind of bread or cake

> Peggy ate a hot **roll.**

• to move by turning over many times; to make flat with a roller

> Ben will **roll** the tire into the garage.
> The dog likes to **roll** in the grass.
> Mother must **roll** the dough for a pie.

roof
the covering on the top of a building

> There is a chimney on the **roof** of this building.

room
a space enclosed by walls in a house or a building; space

> This **room** has one door and three windows.
> There is **room** for you in the car.

root
the part of a plant, usually in the soil, which feeds the plant and holds it in place

A carrot is a **root.**

The **roots** of most trees grow deep in the ground.

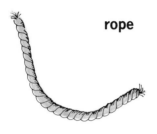

rope
a thick, strong cord made of strings twisted together

The boat is tied to the dock with heavy **rope.**

I have a jump **rope.**

rose
See **Words for Flowers,** page 197.

rot′ ten
spoiled; weak

Jack could not eat the apple, because it was **rotten.**

The old steps are dangerous, because some of the boards are **rotten.**

round
having a shape like a ball or a ring

A baseball is **round.**

A wheel is **round.**

I drew a clown with a **round** face.

row
a line

Children are sitting in the front **row** of chairs.

The flowers grew in a **row.**

row   to move a boat with oars
        Sam can **row** a boat.
        He must pull hard on the oars when he **rows.**

rub′ ber   one of the low-cut coverings worn over the shoes to protect them from water; a stretch material
        Jan wears her **rubbers** when it rains.
        Tires and erasers are made of **rubber.**
        Rubber is made from the juice of a tree.

rul′ er   a straight strip that is used in measuring; one who controls something, such as a country and its people
        A **ruler** is usually twelve inches long.
        The queen was a wise **ruler.**

run   to move fast on the legs; to go
   ran   The children can **run** fast.
   run   A dog **ran** after the children.
   run′ ning   Sarah has **run** in a race.
        The clock is not **running.**

rush   to move fast; to hurry
   rush′ es   I sometimes **rush** to the bus stop.
        A person who is late often **rushes.**

sad
  sad′ ly

unhappy
    The **sad** little girl began to cry.
    She looked **sadly** at the broken doll.

sad′ dle

a seat, usually made of leather, for the rider on a horse or a bicycle
    The rider will put the **saddle** on the horse.

safe
  safe′ ly

free from danger
    We keep our money in a **safe** place.
    Workers fixed the old bridge so that it would be **safe**.
    The airplane landed **safely**.

said

See **say.**

sail

- the cloth on a boat against which the wind blows to move the boat on the water
    The wind puffs out the **sail** on the small boat.

- to travel on water by boat
    In the summer people **sail** on the lake.

salt
salty

a white grain-like seasoning for foods, which is found in the earth and in sea water

Jane filled the shaker with **salt**.

The **salty** peanuts made me thirsty.

same

just alike; not different

The boy's shirts are the **same** color.

Jan's birthday is on the **same** day as mine.

sang

See **sing.**

sat

See **sit.**

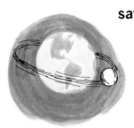

sat′ el lite

a heavenly body that moves around a larger body; an object that is sent into orbit in space

The moon is the earth's **satellite**.

A **satellite** may carry a camera to take pictures of outer space.

Some **satellites** send messages.

save
sav′ ing

to get someone or something out of danger; to keep or to put aside

Lifeguards often **save** people who are drowning.

I will **save** the fruit to eat later.

Judy is **saving** her money.

saw   a tool with sharp teeth that is used for cutting

> Mother used a **saw** to cut the tree trunk into logs.

saw   *See* **see.**

say   to speak; to tell
said
say′ ing
> Please **say** that poem again.
> "Dinner is ready," **said** Father.
> What is the teacher **saying**?

scare   to make afraid
scar′ ing
> Do ghost stories **scare** you?
> Our dog is **scaring** the little child.

school   a place for teaching and learning
> In **school** our teacher helps us learn many things.
> We go to **school** five days a week.

scream   to cry out in a loud, sharp way
> People sometimes **scream** when they are afraid or hurt.

sea   a large body of water; the ocean
> The **sea** is salty.

seal   *See* **Words for Animals,** page 208.

seat something to sit on, such as a chair or a bench

There is an empty **seat** in the first row.

se′ cret something which is known by one or two people, but kept from others

Barbara won't tell anyone the **secret.**

see to sense through the eyes; to look at
  saw   If you open your eyes, you can **see.**
  seen   Andy **saw** dark clouds, and then he heard thunder.
  see′ ing Paula has **seen** the kittens.
  We are **seeing** many new places.

seed the small part of a plant from which new plants grow

I planted a **seed** in some dirt, and now the plant is starting to grow.

seem to look to be
  Does Bill **seem** better?
  He **seems** happier today.

sell to give for a price
  sold   The woman **sells** flowers.
  sell′ ing Tom **sold** his old skates for a dollar.
  We are **selling** tickets to the school play.

send   to cause to go
  sent   I will **send** you a letter.
  send' ing   Aunt Anna **sent** Mark to the store.
               We are **sending** the letter by airmail.

set   • a group
           Mother has a **set** of blue dishes.

          • to put in place
set   I'll **set** the dishes on the table.
set' ting   Jeff **set** the box by the door before he left.
           The gardener is **setting** plants in the ground.

sev' er al   two or more, but not many
           The team has won **several** games.

shade   a somewhat dark place which is not in the
  shady   sunshine
           Let's sit in the **shade** under the big tree.
           It is cooler under the **shady** tree than it is in the bright sun.

shad' ow   shade made by a person, an animal, or some object blocking out the sun or light
           The flagpole casts a long **shadow** on the grass.

shake
shook
shak′ en
shak′ ing

to move up and down or back and forth
I'll **shake** my beach towel to get the sand out.
Diane **shook** the jar of orange juice.
Chris has **shaken** the dusty mop.
Liz was **shaking** her head to mean *no*.

shall
should

I **shall** come if I can.
They **shall** go to bed early even though they don't want to.
Jill asked if she **should** write her cousin a letter.

shark

See **Words for Animals,** page 208.

sharp
sharp′ ly

having a fine cutting edge or a thin point; like a knife
The **sharp** knife cuts the meat easily.
The cold wind feels **sharp** against my cheeks.
The angry woman spoke **sharply.**

she
her
her
hers

the girl, the woman, or the female animal spoken about
She is my aunt.
I am visiting **her.**
I am staying at **her** house.
The green house is **hers.**

sheep
sheep

See **Words for Animals,** page 209.

shell the hard covering on such things as some animals, birds' eggs, and nuts

Meg found a clam's **shell** at the beach.

A turtle can pull its head and its legs into its **shell.**

A robin's egg has a blue **shell.**

The **shell** of a nut is often hard.

shine
shone or
shined
shin' ing

to be bright with light; to make bright

Stars **shine** on a clear night.

I can **shine** shoes well.

The sun **shone** all day.

Beth is **shining** her ring.

shiny bright

A new penny is **shiny.**

ship an object which is larger than a boat and which is used for traveling on deep water

The sailor went to sea on a **ship.**

shirt a piece of clothing worn on the upper part of the body

A **shirt** usually has sleeves and a collar.

shoe a covering for the foot, usually made of leather

A **shoe** fits the shape of a foot.

shook   *See* **shake.**

shoot   to hit with something, such as an arrow
   shot   or a bullet; to move out rapidly
   shoot' ing   In the movies cowboys may **shoot**
at each other.
       Flames **shot** from the fire.
       The men were **shooting** arrows.

shop   • a store where things are sold
       My sister works in a flower **shop.**
       The bakery **shop** has pies for sale.

       • to look at or to buy things in a store
   shopped   People **shop** for food and clothes.
   shop' ping   Mother **shopped** at the supermarket.
       Cynthia was **shopping** for a hat.

shore   the land at the edge of a body of water
       It is rocky along this **shore.**

short   low; not tall; quick; not long
       The grass has been cut **short.**
       The class went for a **short** walk.

shot   *See* **shoot.**

should   *See* **shall.**

shout   to call in a loud voice
            Since Steve is far away, he must **shout** if we are to hear him.

shov′ el   a tool which has a handle and a wide piece or scoop used to dig and throw
            Ann dug into the sand with the **shovel.**
            Bob used a **shovel** to lift the snow.

show   ● a display or a program which can be seen, such as on television or on the stage
            What television **show** do you watch?

            ● to let others look at; to be seen; to teach by doing

showed   Will you **show** us your goldfish?
shown or   The rip in her dress **showed.**
  showed   Mother has **shown** me how to knit.
show′ ing   Dick is **showing** his paper to Dan.

show′ er   a small amount of rain; a bath using a spray of water
            The weatherman said there might be a **shower** today.
            Sometimes I wash my hair when I take a **shower.**

sick   ill; not feeling well
            Tommy is **sick** with the mumps.

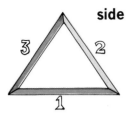

side   an outer line or surface of an object; one of the two parts of something which is not the top, the bottom, the front, or the back; a certain part or place

The figure in the picture has three **sides.**

A bus has a door on one **side.**

We play on this **side** of the street.

sign   ● a mark or a message that points out or means something

Here is a *For Sale* **sign.**

The dark clouds were a **sign** of rain.

We use the $ **sign** to stand for *dollar.*

● to write your own name on

People **sign** their letters.

sig′ nal   an action, a word, or a sign that has a special meaning

The man blew a whistle as a **signal** for the race to begin.

sil′ ly   foolish
sil′ lier
sil′ liest

Jack looked **silly** in his sister's hat.

My picture is **sillier** than yours.

That is the **silliest** show I have seen.

sil′ ver   a shiny white metal

Is your bracelet made of **silver**?

Silver often shines brightly.

sing   to make musical sounds with the voice
  sang   The children **sing** well.
  sung   The bird **sang** sweetly.
  sing′ ing   We have **sung** this song many times.
               Tom is **singing.**

sis′ ter   a girl or a woman who has the same mother and father as another person
               I have one **sister** and two brothers.

sit   to be in a seat
  sat   May I **sit** in the chair next to you?
  sit′ ting   On the bus trip, Mother **sat,** but I stood.
               The cat is **sitting** in a basket.

skate   ● a form for the foot with a metal blade on the bottom for gliding on ice; a form for the foot with rollers on the bottom for gliding on hard, dry places
               The blade on an ice **skate** is thin.
               My roller **skates** have straps that go around the tops of my shoes.

● to glide while wearing ice skates or roller skates
skat′ ing   The children **skate** on the ice-covered pond.
               It is spring, and girls are **skating** on the sidewalk.

skunk	*See* **Words for Animals,** page 209.

sky
skies

the space above the earth
  A clear **sky** is helpful to pilots.
  Stars twinkle in the night **sky.**

sled

a frame which is on runners and which is used for sliding on snow
  Robert will ride his **sled** down the snowy hill.

sleep
slept
sleep′ ing

to rest the mind and the body
  People usually close their eyes when they **sleep.**
  Who **slept** in my bed?
  Timothy is **sleeping** now.

sleepy

needing sleep; tired
  Mother put the **sleepy** girl to bed.

slide
slid
slid′ ing

to move easily and quickly
  Sam likes to **slide** down the long slide at the playground.
  Ed **slid** on the slippery floor.
  The children are **sliding** on the ice.

slip′ pery

causing one to slide and maybe to fall
  A **slippery** floor can be dangerous.

slow
slow′ ly
: taking a long time; behind time
  Since Beth is **slow** in getting ready, she is often late.
  My watch is **slow.**
  The tired children walked **slowly.**

small
: little; not large
  The baby seems **small** next to his father.
  My shoes are too **small.**

smart
: quick to learn
  Kay is **smart,** and she does good work.

smell
: to sense with the nose
  Do you **smell** something burning?

snail
: *See* **Words for Animals,** page 209.

snake
: *See* **Words for Animals,** page 209.

snow
snowy
: frozen water in soft white flakes of different shapes
  Snow fell from the wintry sky.
  I wear my mittens on **snowy** days.

so
: in such a way; very; and for that reason
  Please do not talk **so** loud.
  I am **so** sorry!
  It rained, **so** we could not go.

soft
soft′ ly

not hard or stiff; pleasing to touch; gentle
My pillow is **soft.**
A kitten's fur feels very **soft.**
Our teacher has a **soft** voice.
The mother sang **softly** to her baby.

sold

See **sell.**

sol′ id

not hollow; hard
The block of wood is **solid.**

some

a certain, but not named, being or thing;
a number of; any
Some day next week Janet will visit us.
Some plants bloom, but others do not.
Do you want **some** food?

song

music to be sung
Miss Snow played the piano while the
children sang the **song.**

soon

in a short time; quickly
We will come again **soon.**
As **soon** as Mary comes, we will go.

sor′ ry

sad
I am **sorry** that you are ill.

sound

something received through the sense of
hearing
Jean heard the **sound** of footsteps.

soup   a liquid food which is made by boiling such things as meat, fish, and vegetables in water

       This **soup** is too hot to eat.

south   a direction

       South is the opposite of *north*.
       Mexico is **south** of the United States.

space   a place; an endless area

       There is **space** in the car for you.
       The planets move through **space.**

speak   to talk; to use the voice
spoke   You should **speak** clearly.
spo′ ken   An author **spoke** to our class.
speak′ ing   Mother has **spoken** to my teacher.
       Andy is **speaking** in front of an audience.

spend   to pay out; to use up
spent   David will **spend** a nickel for an apple.
spend′ ing   Kathy **spent** an hour at the library.
       The woman is **spending** money at the grocery store.

spi′ der   *See* **Words for Animals,** page 209.

spin′ ach   *See* **Words for Vegetables,** page 201.

splash
  splash' es

to cause water to fly about
  Chris likes to **splash** in the bathtub.
  The rain **splashes** on the window.

spoke

See **speak.**

spot

a mark; a place
  There is a **spot** of ink on the shirt.
  The cat found a good **spot** for a nap.

spread

to cover a wide area
  If the milk spills, it may **spread** across
the table.

spring

the season between winter and summer;
a small stream of water that bubbles out
of the ground; an elastic part, usually
metal, which will return to its first shape
after it has been forced out of shape
  Spring follows winter.
  Water bubbled from the **spring.**
  A **spring** under the car seat is broken.

squash

See **Words for Vegetables,** page 201.

squir' rel

See **Words for Animals,** page 209.

stair

one of several steps which are used to go
from one level or one floor to another
  The kitten is on the bottom **stair.**

stand
  stood
  stand' ing

to be in place on one's feet
> We **stand** in line for the fire drill.
> The children **stood** up to salute the flag.
> At the game some people are sitting, but the boys are **standing.**

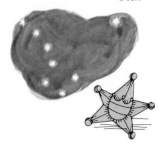

star

a heavenly body which appears bright at night; a shape; a performer who is very good
> Have you ever seen the North **Star?**
> In the movie the sheriff was wearing a silver **star.**
> Bill Jones is the **star** of the school play.

start

to begin to go or to do
> Mother will **start** cooking dinner soon.
> The car won't **start.**

sta' tion

a stopping place for a bus or a train
> This is a bus **station.**
> Trains stop at the train **station.**

stay

to remain in one place
> How long can you **stay?**

steam

water in the form of gas
> **Steam** is coming from the pan of boiling water.

step	to move the foot from one place to
stepped	another; to walk
step′ ping	Don't **step** in the mud puddle.
	Tammy **stepped** onto the bus.
	Pat is **stepping** over the box.

stick   a thin piece of wood; a thin piece
                  The boys gathered **sticks** for the fire.
                  Chris chewed a carrot **stick.**

stick   to push a pointed end into something;
stuck   to make or to be hard to move
stick′ ing   The sharp pin may **stick** you.
                  Kim **stuck** a tack into the wall.
                  Is the stamp **sticking** to the envelope?

still   without moving or making noise
                  We sat **still** during the movie.

sting   to hurt with a pricking feeling
stung   Smoke makes my eyes **sting.**
sting′ ing   A wasp **stung** Marie.
                  The burn on my finger is **stinging.**

stir   to mix; to move
stirred   The painter must **stir** the paint.
stir′ ring   No one **stirred** while Miss Long was
                  out of the room.
                  Uncle Ed is **stirring** the soup.

stone   a piece of rock
                   We have a fireplace made of **stone.**

stood   *See* **stand.**

stop   to keep from moving; to come to an end
  stopped   The policeman will **stop** the cars to
  stop' ping   let us cross the street.
                       It was quiet after the noise **stopped.**
                       The umpire is **stopping** the game
                   because it is raining.

store   a place where many things are kept to
                   sell
                       Jack bought a cap at the department
                   store.

storm   bad weather with strong wind and usually
  stormy   rain, hail, or snow
                       The wind blew hard during the **storm**
                   yesterday.
                       We play in the house on **stormy** days.

sto' ry   a telling of either true or made-up things
  sto' ries   and happenings
                       I read an interesting **story** about the
                   first space trip.

stove   an object which gets power from something, such as gas or electricity, and which is used for cooking and heating
      Mother took the pan of boiling water off the **stove.**

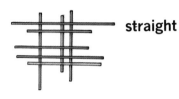

straight   without a bend or a turn
      All the lines are **straight.**
      We went **straight** home.

strange   unusual; not known, heard, or seen before
      Pam had a **strange** dream.
      What is that **strange** animal?

stran' ger   one who is not known
      The **stranger** told people his name.

straw   a dried stem of a grain plant; a tube, usually made of paper, through which one can suck liquids
      Cattle often sleep on beds of **straw.**
      I sipped the soda through a **straw.**

straw' ber ry   *See* **Words for Fruits,** page 199.
straw' ber ries

street   a road in a town or city
      Many cars travel down our **street.**
      A city has many **streets.**

strike   to hit with force; to stop work as a group
  struck   for a reason
  strik′ ing   **Strike** the ball with the bat.
     The workers may **strike,** because they
want better pay.
     A car **struck** a tree.
     The bus drivers are **striking.**

string   very thin rope; very heavy thread
     The package is tied with **string.**
     Betty is putting beads on a **string.**

strong   having power or force
     You must be **strong** to lift the trunk.

struck   *See* **strike.**

stuck   *See* **stick.**

stung   *See* **sting.**

sud′ den   quick
  sud′ den ly   He made a **sudden** movement.
     Suddenly the wind began to blow.

sug′ ar   a sweetening, usually made from sugar
cane or sugar beets
     I put some **sugar** in the lemonade.

suit   clothing worn by a man or a boy that is made up of a matching jacket, pants, and sometimes a vest; a woman's or a girl's matching jacket and skirt

Joe has a blue wool **suit.**

Miss Baker sometimes wears a **suit** instead of a dress.

sum′ mer   the season between spring and fall

It is often hot in the **summer.**

sun   the heavenly body which gives us light
sun′ ny   and heat

The **sun** is shining brightly.
Sunny days are cheerful.

sun′ flow er   *See* **Words for Flowers,** page 197.

sup′ per   an evening meal

When people eat dinner at noon, they have **supper** at night.

sup pose′   to think it is possible

Do you **suppose** the rain will stop?

sure   certain; without a doubt
sure′ ly   I feel **sure** I can win the race.

That man is **surely** Mr. Thomas.

sur prise'   something unexpected
    Mother has a **surprise** for us, and we are trying to guess what it is.

swan   *See* **Words for Animals,** page 209.

sweet   tasting like sugar; pleasant
    Honey tastes **sweet.**
    Roses have a **sweet** smell.
    The baby has a **sweet** smile.

swim   to move oneself forward in the water
swam   without touching the ground or any
swum   bottom surface
swim' ming   You move your arms and your legs when you **swim.**
    The fish **swam** around in the fishbowl.
    Have you ever **swum** in the ocean?
    Ducks are **swimming** in the pond.

swing   to move back and forth
swung   People **swing** their arms when they
swing' ing   walk.
    The door **swung** open and then closed.
    The monkey is **swinging** by his tail.

swish   to move with a hissing sound
swish' es   Leaves often **swish** in the breeze.
    The nurse's stiff dress **swishes** when she walks.

ta′ ble
a piece of furniture having a flat top on legs
The children sat at the **table** to eat their lunch.

tail
A growth from the back of an animal; something like an animal's tail
The dog is wagging its **tail**.
I made a long **tail** of rags for my kite.

take
  took
  tak′ en
  tak′ ing
to get; to go with; to use
May I **take** a pencil from the box?
"Please **take** Chris outdoors," said Mother.
They **took** a bus to the city.
Who has **taken** the last piece of bread?
We are **taking** them to the movies.

tale
a story
I read a fairy **tale**.

talk
to speak; to say words
You should listen when people **talk**.

tall   high

        Some city buildings are very **tall.**
        Henry was short, but he grew to be
tall.

tap   to hit lightly
  tapped   **Tap** gently on the door.
  tap′ ping   Rain **tapped** on the roof.
        Who is **tapping** on the window?

taste   to get the flavor of something by putting
  tast′ ing a small part of it in your mouth
        Mother will **taste** the soup to see if it
is too salty.
        Peter is **tasting** the chocolate pudding.

taxi   an automobile with a special driver, which
people pay to ride in
        When we missed the bus, we had to
take a **taxi** to school.
        The ride in the **taxi** cost a dollar.

teach   to show how to do something; to lead
  teach′ es others to learn
  taught   I will **teach** you a new game.
  teach′ ing My mother **teaches** the first grade.
        Who **taught** you how to ride a bicycle?
        Mrs. Blake is **teaching** our class many
interesting facts about science.

team   a number of people working or playing
                    together
                    Our **team** won the game.

tear   to pull or to rip apart
  tore   How did you **tear** your dress?
  torn   Joe **tore** his shirt on a sharp nail.
  tear′ ing   Someone has **torn** the book jacket.
                        Louis is **tearing** up the old papers.

tear   a drop of salty water from the eye
                    A **tear** ran down the baby's cheek.

teeth   *See* **tooth.**

tel′ e phone   a set which uses electricity to let people
                    who are near or far apart talk to each
                    other
                        My cousin in Chicago called my aunt
                    in Boston on the **telephone.**

tel′ e vi sion a way of sending and receiving pictures
                    and sounds by electrical waves; the set
                    which receives the electrical waves and
                    gives out the pictures and the sounds
                        Television lets people see things that
                    are happening far away.
                        Bob turned on the **television** to watch
                    the ball game.

tell   to say; to let others know
  told   I can't **tell** which book is yours.
  tell' ing   Will you **tell** me the secret?
                    Mother **told** Jim that it was time for
                bed.
                    Mrs. Parker is **telling** us a story.

tem' per a ture   a measure of heat or cold
                    When the air gets warmer, the
                temperature changes.

tent   a movable shelter, usually made of cloth
                and supported by poles in the ground
                    Campers sometimes sleep in a **tent.**

than   when compared to
                    I am older **than** Catherine.

thank   to say that one is pleased about
                something said or done
                    You should **thank** people when they
                are kind to you.

that   pointing out someone or something
                which is farther away or which has been
                spoken about; which
                    I will take **that** book, not this one.
                    We can't stay **that** long.
                    Joan ate the apple **that** was on the
                table.

the	pointing out a certain one or ones **The** girls raced down **the** road.
their **theirs**	belonging to them; a form of *they* The women took off **their** coats. The coats on the hooks are **theirs**.
them	the persons, the animals, or the things spoken about; a form of *they* Judy asked **them** to go with us.
then	at that time; soon afterward Just **then** our doorbell rang. I'll read the book, and **then** you may have it.
there	in that place She sat **there**, instead of here.
these	pointing out persons or things which are nearby Is one of **these** books hers? **These** shoes are bigger than those shoes.

they
  them
  their
  theirs
	the persons, the animals, or the things spoken about
	They are the best players on the team.
	I live near **them**.
	Their aunt is watching the game.
	The caps on the grass are **theirs**.

thick   having a great measure between sides;
not thin; growing or being close together;
like glue

The telephone book for a large city
is very **thick.**

We had fun hiding in the long, **thick**
grass.

The paint is too **thick** to use.

thin   not thick or fat; growing far apart; like
thin′ ner   water
thin′ nest

Lisa is too **thin** to wear this skirt.

Grandfather has **thin** hair.

I made the paste **thinner** by adding
water.

The **thinnest** book is not always the
easiest to read.

thing   an object; an idea; a happening

A desk is a **thing.**

Tim thought of an interesting **thing**
to write about.

A funny **thing** happened today.

think   to use the mind; to have an idea; to have
thought   in mind
think′ ing

People can **think,** but plants cannot.

Peggy **thought** of a game we could
play.

Betty was **thinking** about vacation.

thirsty   wanting something to drink
      The dog is **thirsty** and needs some water.

this   pointing out a person or a thing which is nearby
      This football is Jim's, but that baseball is Andy's.
      This boy is my brother.

those   pointing out persons or things which are far away
      Those people across the street are my parents.
      Which of **those** dolls do you like?

thought   *See* **think.**

threw   *See* **throw.**

through   from one end to the other end of
      This road will take you **through** the city.

throw   to toss
  threw   You **throw** the ball, and I'll catch it.
  thrown   Alice **threw** the empty bag into the
  throw' ing wastebasket.
             I have **thrown** the papers away.
             The children are **throwing** snowballs.

tick′ et   a card or a piece of paper which lets one do something, such as go to a show or ride on a bus

Paul paid for the **ticket** to the game.
Do you have a bus **ticket**?

ti′ ger   *See* **Words for Animals,** page 209.

tight   not easily moved or undone; fitting closely; not loose

Ed can tie a **tight** knot in the rope.
My toes hurt, because my shoes are too **tight.**

time   a measure of years, days, hours, and minutes; a part of a year, day, or hour

Clocks and calendars are two ways of telling **time.**
What **time** do you get to school?.

ti′ ny
ti′ ni er
ti′ ni est   very small

The kittens are **tiny.**
They are **tinier** than the cat.
The gray kitten is the **tiniest** of the three kittens.

tip   an end part which is rounded or pointed

The seal has a ball on the **tip** of his nose.

tip
tipped
tip′ ping

to turn over
    Canoes **tip** easily.
    Who **tipped** over the flowerpot?
    The glass is **tipping**!

tip

a small amount of money given to a person for good service
    Mrs. Burns gave a **tip** to the taxi driver who took her to the airport.

tire

a band of rubber or metal around a wheel
    Each wheel on my bicycle has a rubber **tire.**

tired

worn out; sleepy
    After a long day at work, the men were **tired.**

to

in the direction of; on; for
    Turn **to** the left.
    Does the stamp stick **to** the envelope?
    Jack has the key **to** the front door.

toad

See **Words for Animals,** page 209.

to day′

at the present time
    Today is between yesterday and tomorrow.

to geth′ er   with each other; not alone
      The girls are walking **together.**
      Jack nailed the boards **together.**
      We sat **together** at lunchtime.

told   *See* **tell.**

to ma′ to   *See* **Words for Vegetables,** page 201.
  to ma′ toes

to mor′ row   the day after the present one
      Today is Saturday, and **tomorrow** will
be Sunday.

to night′   the night of today
      I am sleepy **tonight.**

too   also; more than what is enough
      Jane is here, and Ann is, **too.**
      Mark is **too** young to go to school.

took   *See* **take.**

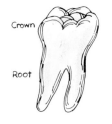

tooth   one of the bony parts in the mouth which
  teeth   are used for biting; something like a tooth,
such as on a comb or a saw
      A **tooth** has a root and a crown.
      Each **tooth** on the saw is sharp.

top
the highest part
> Snow covers the **top** of the mountain.
> Your head is at the **top** of your body.

top
a toy with a pointed end on which it spins
> The **top** turned round and round.

tore
See **tear.**

tor na' do
a very strong wind which whirls around like a cone-shaped cloud
> The **tornado** blew many trees down.

touch
touch' es
to put the hand or some part of the body on something; to come against
> I can bend and **touch** my toes.
> The tree branch **touches** our roof.

toward
in the direction of
> They walked **toward** the park.
> The puppy raced **toward** the boys.

tow' er
a high, narrow building or a high, often narrow part of a building
> A clock is in the **tower.**
> The old castle had a stone **tower.**

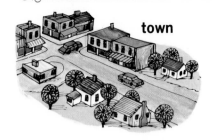

town　　a group of many houses and buildings, which is smaller than a city

There is less traffic in a **town** than in a city.

toy　　a plaything

A puppet is a **toy.**

track　　a row of metal rails for cars to run on; a mark made by a wheel or a foot passing over an area

The train **track** has steel rails.

The dog left muddy **tracks** on the rug.

trac′ tor　　a heavy machine used to pull such things as plows and other machines

The **tractor** pulled our car out of the ditch.

trade
trad′ ing　　to give one thing for another

Will you **trade** books with me?

We **trade** pictures of ballplayers.

Since Tim's chair is too small, he is **trading** it for Jack's bigger chair.

traf′ fic　　the movement of people, cars, and bicycles along streets and roads

There is a lot of **traffic** on this road during the summer.

trail
- a path or a track
  The jet left a **trail** of gases in the sky.

- to follow
  Dogs often **trail** behind a parade.

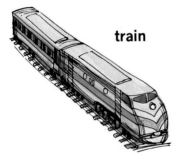

train
- a line of railroad cars which are fastened together and pulled by an engine
  The **train** is coming down the track.

- to teach
  Bill can **train** his dog to do tricks.

trap
something used to catch animals
Father caught a mouse in the **trap.**

trav′ el
to go on a trip
We will **travel** in Canada this summer.

treas′ ure
riches which have been stored up or hidden
The boys pretended they were digging for **treasure** in the sand.

tree
a large, woody plant with a trunk, branches, and leaves
This is a maple **tree.**
A **tree** is the largest kind of plant.

trick   something done to fool people; a clever act

The magician's **trick** made us think that the glass had really disappeared.

Sue taught her dog a **trick** of begging for food.

trip   ● a journey

The class is taking a **trip** to the art museum.

The Greens went on a **trip** last year.

● to stumble; to catch the foot and fall

tripped   You may fall if you **trip.**
trip′ ping   Barbara **tripped** on the rock.

Kim was **tripping** over things in the dark room.

trot   to move like a horse by lifting a front foot
trot′ ted   and the opposite hind foot at the same
trot′ ting   time

We watched the horse **trot.**

The little dog **trotted** down the road.

The pony is **trotting** around the circus ring.

truck   a heavy automobile for carrying loads

The driver put our broken T.V. into the **truck.**

Newspapers were put onto a **truck.**

trunk   the main stem of a tree, not including
the branches and the roots; a large case;
a space, often in the back of a car, for
storing things; the long snout of an
elephant

Bark covers the **trunk** of the tree.

We packed our clothes in a **trunk**.

Mother keeps tools in the **trunk** of
the car.

The elephant can use its **trunk** to
hold things.

try   to attempt
  tries   You should **try** to do your best.
  tried   The baby **tries** to walk.
  try′ ing   I **tried** to open the door, but it was
locked.

Pat is **trying** to go to sleep.

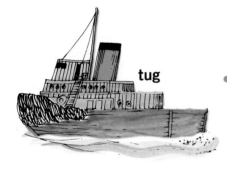

tug   a small boat used to tow and to push
larger boats

The little **tug** pushed the boat.

The large ship was towed into port
by a **tug**.

to pull hard
tugged   The puppy likes to **tug** at the shoe.
tug′ ging   We **tugged** on the rope which was
tied to the boat.

Kathy was **tugging** on the heavy
wagon to make it move.

tu′ lip   *See* **Words for Flowers,** page 197.

tum′ ble   to fall or to turn over
  tum′ bling   If you run, you may **tumble** down
the steps.
    The clothes are **tumbling** about in the
washing machine.

tur′ key   *See* **Words for Animals,** page 210.

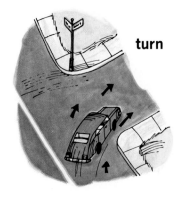

turn   • a change of direction; a chance or a time
to do something
    The car is making a **turn** to the right.
It is Alice's **turn** to swing.

• to move around; to change direction
    When you are riding a bicycle, the
wheels **turn** many times.
    The bus will **turn** left at the corner.

tur′ nip   *See* **Words for Vegetables,** page 201.

tur′ tle   *See* **Words for Animals,** page 210.

twin   one of two children born at the same
time to the same mother
    Ellen is my **twin,** and we look alike.
    Twins do not always look alike.

ug′ ly   not pleasant to look at
   The unkind witch in the movie had an **ugly** face.

um brel′ la   a folding frame covered with cloth and used to protect one from rain or sun
   The red **umbrella** is open, but the blue one is closed.
   The baby sat in the shade under the beach **umbrella.**

um′ pire   a person who sees that the rules are followed in a game, such as baseball
   The **umpire** cried, "You're out!"

un′ cle   the brother of one's father or one's mother; the husband of one's aunt
   My father's brother is my **uncle.**

un′ der   below; lower than
   Ned Jones lives in an apartment **under** ours.
   As the boys watched from above, the boat sailed **under** the bridge.

un til′   up to the time when
                   Mary can stay **until** her parents call.

up   toward the top of; to a higher place
                   Louise is running **up** the stairs.
                   The helicopter began to go **up.**

up on′   on the top of
                   The puppy jumped **upon** the chair.

us   the person speaking and one or more
                   persons spoken about; a form of *we*
                   Jane asked **us** to go camping.
                   Her mother helped **us** put up the tent.

use   to put into action or to work
  us′ ing   May I **use** your pen?
                   Kim is **using** Mother's typewriter.

use′ ful   helpful
                   Old lumber is **useful** for making many
                   things.

usu al   common
  usu al ly   It is not **usual** to have snow in Florida.
                   A police officer **usually** stands on
                   the corner near school.

va ca′ tion   a time of fun and rest from work
　　　We have a long **vacation** from school
in the summer.
　　　Father will have a two-week **vacation.**

val′ en tine   a card or a gift given to a friend or a loved
one on St. Valentine's Day, February 14
　　　Elizabeth pasted a red heart on the
valentine she made for her mother.

val′ ley   the low land between hills or mountains
　　　From the top of the hill, we could see
the **valley** below.
　　　A river flows through the **valley.**

vase   a holder for flowers
　　　Miss Baker put the daisies in a green
glass **vase.**

veg′ e ta ble   a plant having some part which is used
for food
　　　Beans are my favorite **vegetable.**

very

truly; greatly

Mrs. Gordon is a **very** kind woman.

The Statue of Liberty is **very** tall.

vil′ lage

a small town

There are only a few stores in the **village.**

vi′ o let

See **Words for Flowers,** page 197.

vis′ it

to come or to go to see; to stay with

"Shall we **visit** Uncle Harry today?" asked Mrs. Howe.

My cousin may **visit** us for a week.

vis′ i tor

one who goes to see a person or a place

George had many **visitors** when he was in the hospital.

voice

the sound which comes through the mouth of a person talking or singing

Father speaks in a deep **voice.**

vow′ el

an open sound made by the voice; a letter of the alphabet that stands for an open sound made by the voice

The letters *a, e, i, o,* and *u* are **vowels.**

Sometimes the letter *y* is a **vowel,** as in the word *bicycle.*

wag' on
a four-wheeled cart for carrying loads
Robert is putting the bag into the **wagon.**
The horses pulled the farm **wagon.**

wait
to stop; to stay until someone comes or until something happens
"**Wait** for me," Jenny called as she ran after the boys.
I will **wait** for the rain to stop.

walk
● a path or place for traveling, usually on foot
We played by the **walk** in front of our apartment building.

● to go by foot
Peggy will **walk,** but I will ride.

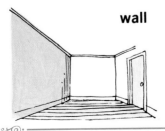

wall
the side of a building or a room; something that encloses an area
One **wall** in the room is green.
A cat walked on the **wall** between our yard and the neighbor's yard.

wal′ rus   *See* **Words for Animals,** page 210.
wal′ rus or **wal′ rus es**

want   to wish for; to need
                   Marie and Sara **want** summer to come.
                   Do you **want** anything at the store?

warm   having some heat; more hot than cold
                   Ann felt the **warm** sun on her back.

warn   to let one know ahead of time of a danger
                   or an unpleasant happening
                       Did you **warn** the boys that the ice is
                   too thin to skate on?
                       Weathermen **warn** us about storms.

was   a form that is used to show past time
                   (Use with *I, he, she, it,* and words that
                   mean only one.)
                       I **was** in bed early last night.
                       He **was** in Susan's class last year.
                       Miss Smith **was** at school yesterday.
                       The sun **was** shining.

wash   to clean with water or some other liquid
  wash′ es   You should **wash** your hands when
                   they are dirty.
                       My sister **washes** her sweaters in
                   cold water.

wasp   *See* **Words for Animals,** page 210.

watch   ● a small clock, usually worn on the wrist
watch' es   A **watch** is often run by a small spring.

                   ● to pay attention to; to look at
                       We **watch** our teacher when she is
                   explaining something to us.
                       Ron **watches** television after dinner.

wa' ter   the liquid that fills lakes, oceans, and
                   rivers and comes from the sky as rain
                       People use **water** for drinking and
                   washing.
                       Land and **water** cover the earth.

wa' ter mel on   *See* **Words for Fruits,** page 199.

wave   ● a moving ripple of water; moving energy
                       in the air, such as sound or light
                       A **wave** splashed against the side of
                   the boat.
                       Sound travels through the air by
                   means of **waves.**

                   ● to move something, such as the hand,
                       up and down or back and forth
wav' ing   People **wave** good-by to each other.
                       The boy is **waving** his hand.

way   direction; plan; distance
Which **way** should we go?
I thought of a new **way** to play the game.
It is a long **way** from my house to your house.

we
us
our
ours   the person who is speaking and one or more persons
We are glad you came.
You should visit **us** often.
Have you seen **our** new kittens?
The dog is **ours,** too.

weak   not strong; easily broken
Chris is too **weak** to lift the box.
The baby's cries were **weak.**
The **weak** bridge may break under the heavy truck.

wear
wore
worn
wear′ ing   to have on the body
Sue will **wear** her blue jacket today.
Miss Clark **wore** a flower on her suit.
Has Alice **worn** that hat before?
The man is **wearing** a red shirt.

weath′ er   the condition of the air outside
When the **weather** is stormy, the air is often windy and cool.
On the desert the **weather** is hot and dry.

weave
wove
wo' ven
weav' ing

to make something, such as cloth, by putting threads over and under each other

The woman is using a loom to **weave** the cloth.

Raymond **wove** a basket from strips of straw.

The spider has **woven** a web.

I am **weaving** a potholder.

wee

very tiny

A hummingbird is a **wee** bird.

week

the seven days between Sunday and Saturday; any seven days, one right after another

Saturday is the last day of the **week.**

We will go to the game in a **week.**

weigh

to find out how heavy something is; to have as weight

You stand on the scales if you want to **weigh** yourself.

The suitcases **weigh** fifty pounds.

wel' come
wel' com ing

to greet or to receive happily

Our neighbors **welcome** us home after we have been away.

Jeff is **welcoming** the visitors.

well
bet′ ter
best

in a good way
You did your work **well.**
Al writes **better** than he did.
Shirley writes **best** of all.

well

a hole dug in the ground to get gas, oil, or water
Oil is being pumped from the **well.**
The **well** is deep in the ground.

went

See **go.**

were

a form that is used to show past time (Use with *you, we, they,* and words that mean more than one.)
You **were** at the party, and he was, too.
We **were** sick, but they **were** in school.
The children **were** reading.

west

a direction; where the sun seems to set
East is the opposite of **west.**
Follow the highway **west** of the city.

wet
wet′ ter
wet′ test

soaked or covered with water or another liquid; not dry
My shoes are **wet.**
Is the fresh paint still **wet**?
His mittens are **wetter** than yours.
This is the **wettest** month of the year.

whale   *See* **Words for Animals,** page 210.

wharf   a platform along the shore where ships
wharves   load and unload
or **wharfs**   Boats stop alongside the **wharf** to
unload and to pick up cargo.
People fished from the **wharf.**

what   which thing or things; which
What did you have for lunch?
I asked Jill **what** book she read.

wheat   a grain from which flour, cereals, and
other foods are made
When **wheat** is ripening, it looks like
long, golden grass.

wheel   a round frame that turns on a center pin
A tricycle has three **wheels.**

when   at what time; at the time that
When can you come?
We will go **when** they come.

where   at what place; in the place that
Where do you live?
Judy put the paper **where** it belongs.

which   what one; that
                   Which cap is yours?
                   I read the story **which** you wrote.

while   during the time that
                   I slept **while** it rained.
                   While Al was talking, we were quiet.

whip   to beat
  whipped   It is unkind to **whip** a dog.
  whip′ ping   The rider lightly **whipped** the horse so
                   that it would go faster.
                   The rain is **whipping** against the sails.

whis′ per   to speak in a soft voice
                   We must **whisper** so that we won't
                   awaken the baby.
                   Will you **whisper** the secret to me?

whis′ tle   to make a shrill sound by blowing air
  whis′ tling through a small opening
                   I can **whistle** many songs.
                   James was **whistling** while he was
                   walking to school.

who   what person or persons
  whom   **Who** did that?
  whose   To **whom** did you speak?
                   Whose jacket is this?

whole having all its parts; not just a part of
The apple is **whole,** and the peach is cut into pieces.
We ate the **whole** pie.

why for what reason
Why did you do that?
Tell me **why** you are crying.

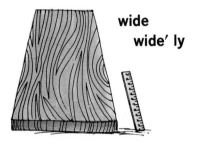

wide
wide′ ly having a great measure from side to side; not narrow
The board is **wide,** and the ruler is narrow.
The ocean is so **wide** that we can't see the other shore.
A famous person is **widely** known.

wife
wives a married woman
Mother is Father's **wife.**

wild
wild′ ly not tame; growing or being without direction
Animals in the jungle are **wild.**
Sometimes flowers grow **wild** along the railroad track.
The lion raged **wildly** in the cage.

will
would I **will** go to school tomorrow.
Ann **will** sing a song in the show.
The boys **will** visit Pete.
He **would** have been gone by then.

win
won
win′ ning

to do better than others in a game or a contest
> The blue boat will **win** the race.
> Jill **won** first prize in the art show.
> We are **winning** the game.

wind
windy

moving air
> The **wind** blows the clothes on the line.
> People must hold onto their hats on **windy** days.

wind
wound
wind′ ing

to wrap around or to roll up; to turn a part of a machine to tighten the spring that makes it go
> I'll **wind** the yarn into a ball.
> Mother **wound** her watch.
> Alice is **winding** the string around the box.

win′ dow

an opening in a wall which lets in light and usually air
> Sunlight shines through the **window.**

wing

the part of a bird, a flying insect, or a bat which is needed for flying; any part which is like a wing, as on an airplane
> A bird has two **wings.**
> The toy airplane has a broken **wing.**

wink
to close and open one eye quickly, usually as a signal

Sometimes Grandfather will **wink** at me when he is joking.

win' ter
the season between fall and spring

Last **winter** was very cold.

Some places have snow in the **winter.**

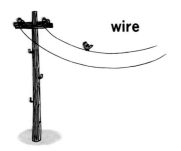

wire
a thin piece of metal which is like thread or cord

A bird is sitting on the telephone **wire.**

There are many electrical **wires** inside our television set.

wise
wise' ly
having and showing good sense

You are **wise** to get a good night's sleep.

I try to spend my money **wisely.**

wish
wish' es
to want

I **wish** I had a brother.

Mel **wishes** he lived in Colorado.

with
in the company of; by means of

Will you come **with** me?

I cut the bread **with** a knife.

wolf
wolves   *See* **Words for Animals,** page 210.

wom′ an
wom′ en   a grown-up girl
        That **woman** is my aunt.

won′ der   to wish to know
        Do you **wonder** what the surprise will be?

won′ der ful   very fine; strangely exciting
        This is a **wonderful** party!
        The astronauts must see **wonderful** things in outer space.

wood   the hard part under the bark of trees, which has many uses when cut
        Tables and chairs are often made of **wood.**

wood′ chuck *See* **Words for Animals,** page 210.

woods   many trees growing wild and close together
        Wildflowers bloom in the **woods.**
        The **woods** do not grow as thick as a forest.

wool
wool′ ly

the soft covering from a sheep which can be made into threads for cloth

The **wool** is cut from the sheep.

My coat is made of **wool.**

The **woolly** blanket was heavy and warm.

word

a sound or a group of sounds which is made by the human voice and which has meaning; a letter or a group of letters which is written to stand for a sound or a group of sounds that has meaning

How many sounds can you hear in that **word**?

There are usually both vowels and consonants in a **word.**

wore

See **wear.**

work

anything which a person does to make a thing or to bring a plan to an end; a job or business

After I do my **work,** I can play.

Mother leaves for **work** at seven o'clock.

world

the earth; the planet on which we live

Our **world** is very large.

The astronauts saw the **world** from their spaceship.

worm   See **Words for Animals,** page 210.

wor′ ry   to be uneasy or troubled
  wor′ ries   Father may **worry** if we are not home
  wor′ ried   on time.
  wor′ ry ing   Mother **worries** about our old car.
                  We **worried** about our sick friend.
                  Are you **worrying** about the storm?

would   See **will.**

wound   See **wind.**

wreck   to break apart or to damage
                  The workers must **wreck** the old
                  building.
                  Drivers must be careful, or they may
                  wreck their cars.

write   to make letters or words with a marker,
  wrote   such as a pen, a pencil, or chalk
  writ′ ten   Laura will **write** her name on the top
  writ′ ing   line of the paper.
                  The teacher **wrote** a sentence on the
                  chalkboard.
                  Have you **written** a letter to Jane?
                  Pat is **writing** a letter.

wrong   bad; not right; not as it should be
                  It is **wrong** to tell a lie.
                  Only one of my answers was **wrong.**

X ray

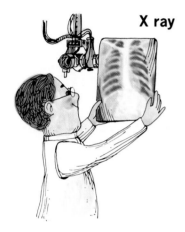

a powerful ray which cannot be seen and which can go through things that light cannot; a picture, often of some area inside the body, which is taken by means of this ray

A special machine uses **X rays.**

The doctor showed us the **X ray** of a man's chest.

xy′ lo phone

a musical instrument which is played with wooden hammers

This is a **xylophone.**

The boy knows how to play a song on the **xylophone.**

Can *you* think of any other words that begin with the letter **X**?

yard

a piece of ground around a house, a school, or some other building

We have a **yard** behind our house.
There is a set of swings in the **yard** at school.

yard

a measure of length

There are three feet in a **yard.**

yawn

to open the mouth wide when one is sleepy or bored

I **yawn** when I am tired.

year

the time from January 1 to December 31; any twelve months, one right after another

There are twelve months in a **year.**
The new school will be built in a **year.**

yell

to scream or to shout

We **yell** and cheer when our favorite team is winning.

yes   a word used in an answer to mean *that is right*

"**Yes,** I can hear you," Margaret answered.

Yes is the opposite of *no.*

yes′ ter day   the day before today

Yesterday was the last day of April, and today is the first day of May.

yet   at this time

I hope you won't go **yet.**

Is Jerry home from school **yet**?

you   the person or the persons spoken to
  you   **You** are reading a dictionary.
  your   Who gave it to **you**?
  yours   There are other children in **your** class.

Which desk is **yours**?

young   in the first part of life

Young is the opposite of *old.*

A calf is a **young** cow.

your   belonging to you; a form of *you*
  yours   Is this **your** desk?

This is my hat, and that is **yours.**

ze′ bra   *See* **Words for Animals,** page 210.

ze′ ro   0; nothing; the point between *1* and —*1* on a thermometer

If you add **zero** to one, you still have one.

The temperature is below **zero,** and the air feels very cold.

zig′ zag   having a shape of short, sharp turns

The jack-o'-lantern has a **zigzag** smile.

Cars go slowly along the **zigzag** road.

zoo   a place where animals are kept in cages or in fenced places so that people can see them

We like to see the lions in the **zoo.**

Word Lists
for
My Second Picture Dictionary

	PAGE
Words for the Space Age	190
Compound Words	191
Antonyms (Word Opposites)	192
Homonyms	193
Kinds of Workers	194
Words for Flowers	196
Words for Fruits	198
Words for Vegetables	200
Words for Animals	202
Birds	211
Dogs	214
Words for Colors	216
Number Words	217
The Days of the Week	217
The Months and Some Important Days	218

Words for the Space Age

aerospace	gravity	reentry
astronaut	launch pad	rocket
booster	lift-off	satellite
capsule	missile	spaceship
countdown	nose cone	space station
escape hatch	orbit	space suit
flight	outer space	thrust
gantry	recovery	weightlessness

Compound Words

airplane	highway	raincoat
baseball	home run	roller skate
basketball	homework	sailboat
bedroom	ice cream	sea horse
beehive	jack-in-the-box	seashore
classroom	jack-o'-lantern	shoemaker
cowboy	jump rope	shopkeeper
doorknob	lighthouse	sidewalk
firecracker	moonlight	snowball
fire escape	newspaper	stop sign
fireman	playground	sunshine
fishhook	police dog	toothache
football	policeman	traffic light
goldfish	postman	washing machine
good-by	post office	windshield
grown-up	railroad	workbook
high school	rainbow	wristwatch

Antonyms

(Word Opposites)

glad

sad

above	below		fat	thin
back	front		few	many
bad	good		first	last
beneath	over		frown	smile
closed	open		hard	soft
cold	hot		heavy	light
dark	light		long	short
dry	wet		loose	tight
dull	sharp		lose	win
early	late		new	old
empty	full		poor	rich
false	true		right	wrong
far	near		rough	smooth
fast	slow		short	tall

Homonyms

hair

hare

ate	eight		mail	male	
bare	bear		meat	meet	
be	bee		pair	pear	pare
blew	blue		peace	piece	
brake	break		red	read	
buy	by		right	write	
cent	scent	sent	sail	sale	
dew	do	due	sea	see	
fair	fare		sew	sow	so
hear	here		son	sun	
hour	our		tail	tale	
knew	new		their	there	
knot	not		threw	through	
made	maid		to	two	too

193

Kinds of Workers

artist

bricklayer

dentist

baker

chemist

doctor

banker

clerk

electrician

forest ranger

musician

cat dog

teacher

judge

nurse

truck driver

mail carrier

plumber

veterinarian

195

Words for Flowers

aster

daffodil

hibiscus

carnation

daisy

Indian paintbrush

crocus

geranium

iris

marigold

poinsettia

sunflower

orchid

pansy

poppy

tulip

petunia

rose

violet

197

Words for Fruits

apple

blackberry

blueberry

date

apricot

cantaloupe

grape

banana

cherry

grapefruit

kumquat

peach

plum

lemon

pear

raspberry

strawberry

orange

pineapple

watermelon

199

Words for Vegetables

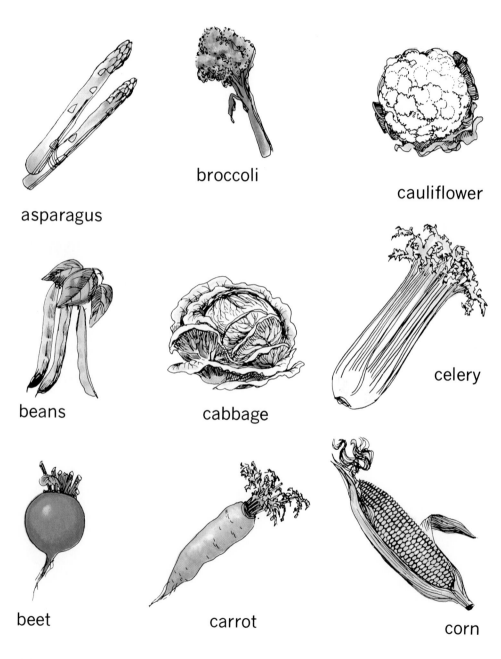

asparagus

broccoli

cauliflower

beans

cabbage

celery

beet

carrot

corn

200

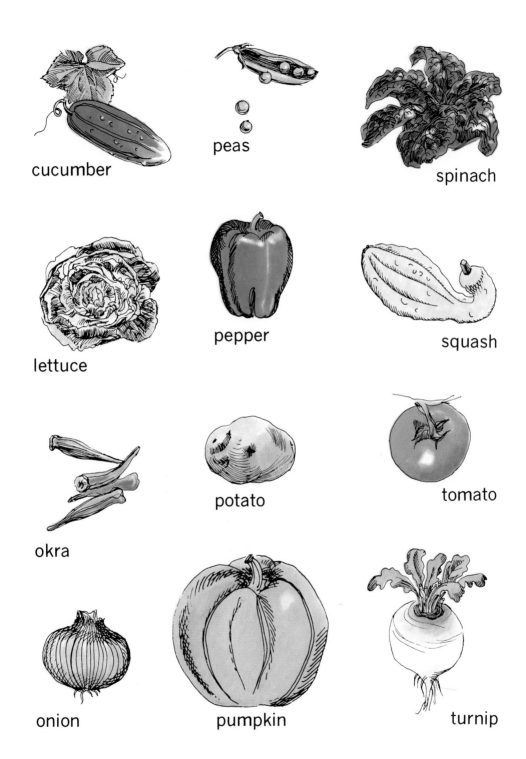

cucumber

peas

spinach

lettuce

pepper

squash

okra

potato

tomato

onion

pumpkin

turnip

201

Words for Animals

alligator

bat

bee

ant

bear

beetle

antelope

beaver

See **Birds,**
page 211.

bird

buffalo

camel

chimpanzee

butterfly

cat

chipmunk

calf

chicken

clam

cow

cricket

See **Dogs**, page 214.

dog

deer

dolphin

coyote

donkey

crab

dinosaur

duck

fly

giraffe

elephant

goat

fox

fish

frog

goose

205

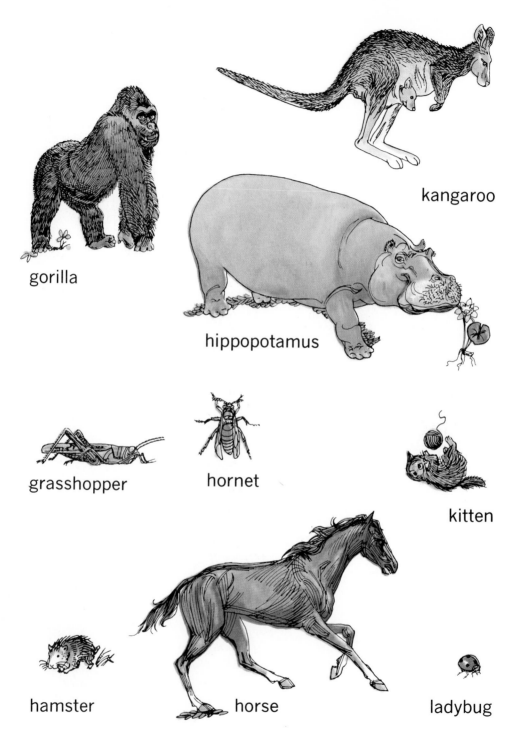

kangaroo

gorilla

hippopotamus

grasshopper

hornet

kitten

hamster

horse

ladybug

lizard

mosquito

lamb

lobster

mouse

leopard

lion

monkey

octopus

opossum

pony

rat

puppy

rhinoceros

penguin

rabbit

seal

pig

raccoon

shark

208

snake

sheep

spider

swan

skunk

tiger

snail

squirrel

toad

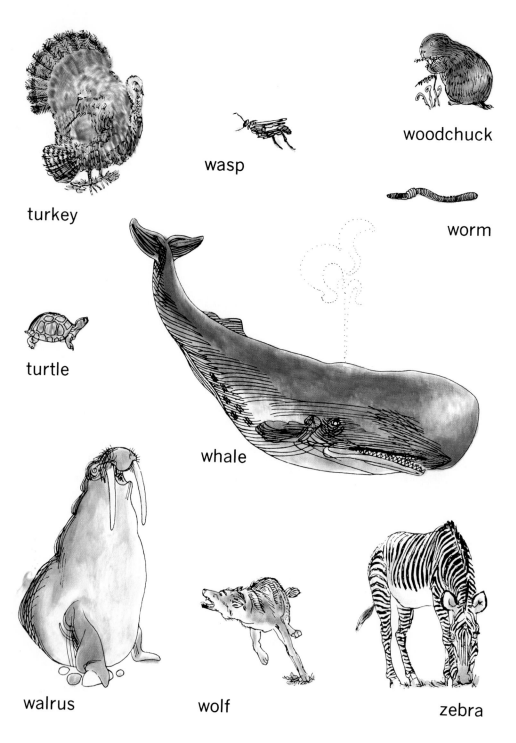

turkey

wasp

woodchuck

worm

turtle

whale

walrus

wolf

zebra

Birds

bluebird

cardinal

eagle

blue jay

chickadee

goldfinch

canary

crow

gull

mockingbird

parakeet

hawk

oriole

parrot

hummingbird

owl

meadowlark

peacock

pheasant

robin

whippoorwill

pigeon

sparrow

woodpecker

roadrunner

thrasher

wren

Dogs

Basset Hound

Bulldog

Collie

Beagle

Chihuahua

Dachshund

Boxer

Cocker Spaniel

Dalmatian

214

German Shepherd

Husky

Saint Bernard

Great Dane

Pointer

Setter

Greyhound

Poodle

Sheepdog

Words for Colors

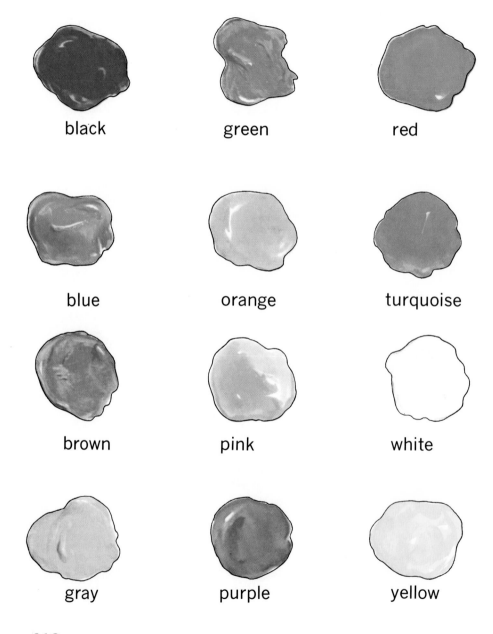

black   green   red

blue   orange   turquoise

brown   pink   white

gray   purple   yellow

Number Words

1	one	first		7	seven	seventh
2	two	second		8	eight	eighth
3	three	third		9	nine	ninth
4	four	fourth		10	ten	tenth
5	five	fifth		11	eleven	eleventh
6	six	sixth		12	twelve	twelfth

The Days of the Week

Sunday	Sun.	Thursday	Thurs.
Monday	Mon.	Friday	Fri.
Tuesday	Tues.	Saturday	Sat.
Wednesday	Wed.		

The Months and Some Important Days

January	February	March
Jan.	Feb.	Mar.
New Year's Day	Lincoln's Birthday Valentine's Day Washington's Birthday	St. Patrick's Day

April	May	June
Apr.		
	Mother's Day	Father's Day

July Fourth of July	August Aug.	September Sept. Labor Day
October Oct. Halloween	November Nov. Thanksgiving Day	December Dec. Christmas Hanukkah

To Parents and Teachers

MY SECOND PICTURE DICTIONARY has been designed to help children learn more about the words they use every day. The words in the dictionary were selected on the basis of word studies by Horn, Rinsland, and Buckingham—Dolch. Another important source was the authors' study of high-frequency words from the compositions of primary-grade children. The contents and format of the book have been planned to help children develop basic dictionary skills while expanding their understanding of language.

The first part of the book presents 1060 alphabetically-arranged entry words with definitions and illustrative sentences. Over one-half of the entries have full-color pictures to expand the children's understanding of the words. Throughout, there is a close correlation between the definition, the sentences, and the illustration for each entry word.

Most of the entry words are divided into syllables. The syllables indicate where a word can be divided at the end of a line in writing. If a word should not be divided because of a one-letter syllable at the beginning or end, it is shown solid (e.g., **about**). Stress marks are used as aids to pronunciation. The stress mark is not used, however, if the stressed syllable should not be written separately (e.g., **usu al**).

Many entry words have subentries to show how a word may change in form. The plural form of a noun is given as a subentry if it is formed in a way other than by adding *s*. The forms of a verb are given as subentries if they are not regularly formed. Other subentries include some common adjectives that are formed from nouns (e.g., **muddy**) and adverbs that are derived from adjectives (e.g., **gently**). Through such presentations, the children develop an understanding of the changes in forms of word classes as they examine these inflectional endings and suffixes.

When a word frequently serves as more than one part of speech, each meaning is indicated by a blue dot. To provide the children with a consistent pattern, noun definitions are given before verb definitions for multi-meaning entries.

In addition to the entries with definitions, nearly 200 cross-references are included in the main part of the dictionary. These cross-references help the children to locate the main forms of words, such as the irregular past tense verbs (e.g., **ate** *See* **eat**.) and commonly used irregular noun plurals (e.g., **men** *See* **man**.). Other cross-references direct the children to the illustrated word lists for animals, flowers, fruits, and vegetables at the back of the dictionary.

The word lists for MY SECOND PICTURE DICTIONARY show the children how words can be classified, since the lists are subject-centered. Included are antonyms, homonyms, compound words, and words for the space age. There are pages for the days of the week, the months and some important days, number words, colors, and kinds of workers. The classification lists are heavily illustrated to aid the children in learning more about the words.